CW00547338

NUTS!

by Sonia Allison

A Cookery Book for Nut Lovers

BELL & HYMAN

London

First published 1984 by
Bell & Hyman Limited
Denmark House
37-39 Queen Elizabeth Street
London SE1 2QB

© Sonia Allison 1984

All rights reserved. No part of this publication may
be reproduced, stored in a retrieval system, or
transmitted in any form or by any means,
electronic, mechanical, photocopying, recording or
otherwise, without the prior permission of
Bell & Hyman Ltd.

Designed by Norman Reynolds

ISBN 0 7135 2406 5

British Library Cataloguing in Publication Data
Allison, Sonia
  Nuts!
  1, Cookery (Nuts)
  I. Title
  641.6'45   TX814

Typeset by Typecast Ltd., Maidstone.
Printed and bound by The Pitman Press Ltd., Bath.

Contents

Nuts plus more nuts

Nuts may not be everyone's crunch, but they certainly appeal to the vast majority who now buy them on a regular basis right through the year, rather than keep them under wraps until the Christmas revelry and feasting begin and conclude already gargantuan meals with a decanter of port in one hand and a pair of nut crackers in the other.

Each and every nut has its own unmistakable shape, character, personality, taste, colour texture and country of origin. Some are vastly expensive, like pistachios and pine nuts, others less so like peanuts. All are nutritious, offering appreciable amounts of body-building protein; energy-giving and unsaturated fats (mostly linoleic acid which is said to reduce cholesterol); important trace elements such as phosphorus, calcium, iron, potassium and magnesium; vitamins of the B group to reduce life's tensions and vitamin E for good skin and longevity (theories as yet unproven). Nuts also contain healthy amounts of fibre so, all in all, bright-eyed vegetarians have a lot going for them.

However, my book is not directed only at health food enthusiasts as I believe nuts have a much wider rôle to play in the culinary lives of ordinary mortals. They offer untold delights when combined with meat, fish, eggs, cheese and vegetables; conjour-up magical flavours woven into desserts and cakes; tantalise the taste buds in appetisers and sauces. A wealth of novelties await but first, a curriculum vitae of each with a final comment before the world jumps upon me. Peanuts are actually a legume (like peas and beans) but slotted into the nut category for convenience. Macadamia nuts, absolutely marvellous and utterly irresistible, are so rare over here and so expensive that they have been excluded from the book altogether. However, if you would like to try them and share with me one of my most delicious gastronomic pleasures, spend your next holiday in Hawaii or Austrialia. Or, nearer home, in the cocktail lounges and bars of Hamburg's Four Seasons Hotel where bowls of Macadamias are proffered with the drinks. Such luxury!

Sonia Allison
Hertfordshire 1984

Almonds

Sweet almonds have been eaten and enjoyed since early biblical times and are mentioned in the Old Testament. They grow on trees native to southern Europe which burst into magnificent pink and white blossoms before the almonds appear. They can be found practically worldwide and are used not only as a food but also for cosmetic purposes: sweet almond oil is often incorporated into beauty preparations for body and hair. Shelled almonds are covered in brown skins, easily removed by blanching. The nuts are pale cream in colour, crisp, almost milky and delicately-flavoured. They form the basis of marzipan. Extract of bitter almonds, another variety of the same nut, is used for essences and extracts after heat treatment. Uncooked bitter almonds contain prussic acid and are poisonous.

Brazils

Named after their country of origin where they are hardly eaten at all, brazils grow on very tall trees, neatly clustered inside large, coconut-like shells which can weigh up to 3 to 4 lb (1.5 to 2 kg) each. The seeds inside are the actual wedge-shaped brazil nuts which, in turn, are surrounded by very tough outer shells. The nuts have been greatly enjoyed in Europe since the middle of the seventeenth century and reached their heyday in Britain during the reign of Victoria. They have a unique and unmistakable flavour with a rich, creamy texture. They harmonise well with both sweet and savoury dishes.

Cashews

Growing on tropical trees native to Brazil, cashews are at their most prolific in India from where they are exported internationally and used in Eastern and Asiatic cooking. They have been known in Europe since the sixteenth century when members of the Portuguese navy took them home from their Indian colonies and called them caju, ultimately translated into cashew. The curvy nuts, shaped like fat little quarter moons, are mild and gentle with a subtle sweetness. They are versatile in cooking and make an appetising snack when roasted and salted. They are always sent to us shelled as their 'overcoats' can cause skin eruptions.

Chestnuts

More starchy and floury than most other nuts and lower in fat, chestnuts are the edible fruit of the sweet chestnut tree, native to the Mediterranean and related to the oak and beech. (Do not confuse these chestnuts with inedible horse chestnuts.) The finest varieties come from Spain and France and marrons glacés are a very expensive and highly-esteemed French sweetmeat, popular around Christmas time. Chestnuts have all manner of sweet and savoury uses and are one of the few nuts which need to be cooked before use. Dried chestnuts are becoming more readily available and, once soaked overnight in water, swell to twice their original weight. Chestnut flour is used in southern Europe for baking.

Coconut

This is a versatile nut which is the fruit of a tropical palm, once native to Malaya. The outer fibrous coating is converted into coconut matting, the flesh is eaten either fresh or dried, and the milk makes a delicious, cooling and healthy drink. In addition to cooking, coconut oil is used in soap, cosmetics and some margarines. A coconut is a large nut and, though imported, economically priced. Fresh grated coconut makes a superb additive to curry dishes. Dried desiccated coconut is much used in baking and in anglicised oriental cooking.

Hazelnuts

Well-loved throughout the world and widely used in the lavish Cream Torten of northern Europe, hazelnuts

grow contentedly on little trees in both Western and Eastern hemispheres, providing small but distinguished nuts for cooking and eating. To remove their somewhat tenacious skins which lie directly beneath the shells, the nuts should be roasted for about 20 minutes in a moderate oven and then rubbed between the hands protected by oven gloves. The skins will flake off easily. In the USA, hazelnuts are known as cobs or filberts.

Peanuts

Like a set of twins, peanuts mature together in light-coloured shells which are flaky and easy to break. Resembling beans in appearance, they came originally from South America and were introduced to the world via Portuguese and Spanish explorers. Peanuts grow below the ground on very fine twigs and nutritionally are an important legume and a good source of protein. They are adaptable in cooking whether used plain or salted and are the least costly of all nuts. The term ground nuts, sometimes used to decribe peanuts, comes from the way they grow under the soil. Peanut oil is widely used and known also as arachis.

Pecans

Pecan nuts are the stones of fruit growing on hickory trees and are native to the southern states of the USA. They resemble oblong walnuts with smooth, thin and reddish-brown shells. The flesh of the nutmeats is slightly wrinkled with a mild and distinguished flavour. Pecans may be used in exactly the same way as walnuts though they have greater delicacy. They are expensive both here and in the United States.

Pine Nuts

Pine nuts are found inside cones growing on pine nut trees (pignolias) in areas of the southern Mediterranian and the USA. They are always sold shelled, are very expensive and have a distinctive, rich flavour and almost wax-like consistency. They are very popular in Middle and Far Eastern cooking and also widely used in the Mediterranean. Italy's famous Pesto, a sauce-like condiment for pasta and minestrone, is based on pine nuts and basil. The nuts themselves are longish and narrow but still quite small.

Pistachios

Native to Syria, pistachios are also cultivated in other areas of the Middle East, the Balkans, Italy and the USA. Esteemed for their vivid green colour and very subtle perfume, the nuts are related to cashews and are the seeds of fruits grown on small trees, Latin name, *Pistacia vera*. They are contained in pale, creamy white shells which have natural splits at one end. Like almonds, pistachios need blanching to remove their skins. They are very expensive and more readily available roasted and salted (in their shells) than they are raw.

Walnuts

Very popular indeed worldwide, walnuts are the stones of fruits of the Juglans regia tree, native to the Middle East but now grown all over Europe and North America. The deep beige shells have a natural split line all the way round each and the nutmeats themselves are crinkled in such a way that they have been likened in appearance to the worried look on a Basset hound or the human brain! American walnuts have dark skins surrounding the white flesh, very hard shells and a strong flavour; European nuts are milder and sweet-tasting. When fresh, they are referred to as green walnuts and sometimes pickled, turning almost black in colour and served with cold meat and cheese.

APPETISERS

Mexican Rose Almonds
Makes about ½lb or 225 g

As Mexican food is taking off in such a big way, what could be more appropriate than these spicy buttered almonds to nibble with drinks as a prelude to a Mexican meal?

8 oz (225 g) blanched almonds
2 oz (50 g) butter or margarine
2 tsp salad oil
2 level tsp chili seasoning (mahogany-coloured and made by Schwarz and McCormick)
½ level tsp salt

1. Make sure almonds are thoroughly dry by rubbing with a tea towel.

2. Fry gently in butter or margarine and oil until they turn pale gold, turning frequently.

3. Remove from pan and drain on crumpled kitchen paper. Afterwards tip on to a clean piece of paper and sprinkle with the chili seasoning and salt.

Devilled Walnuts

Fry 8 oz (225 g) walnut halves as directed in previous recipe. After draining, sprinkle with 2 level teaspoons hot curry powder mixed with ½ level teaspoon paprika, ¼ level teaspoon cayenne pepper and ¼ level teaspoon powder mustard.

Cream Cheese and Gherkin 'Truffles'
Makes 12

Rich, wholesome and a delicious snack.

4 oz (125 g) cream cheese (such as Philadelphia)
1 level tblsp soured cream
1 level tblsp chopped gherkins
2 oz (50 g) red Cheshire cheese, finely grated
salt and pepper to taste
1 oz (25 g) hazelnuts, finely chopped

1. Beat cream cheese smoothly with soured cream. Stir in gherkins and the Cheshire cheese.

2. Season to taste with salt and pepper then roll into 12 truffle shapes. Coat with nuts, spear each with a cocktail stick and refrigerate until firm before serving.

Cream Cheese and Olive 'Truffles'
Makes 12

Make exactly as above, substituting stoned and chopped black olives for the gherkins.

14

Mixed Cheese and Nut Football

Serves about 12 to 16

Fun for a party and teams well with cream crackers.

1 lb (450 g) cream cheese
4 oz (125 g) Lymeswold or other soft blue cheese
4 oz (125 g) mild Cheddar cheese, very finely grated
2 oz (50 g) blanched almonds, toasted to warm gold, very finely chopped
¼ level tsp cayenne pepper
1 garlic clove, peeled and crushed (optional)
½ pt (275 ml) measuring jug, lightly filled with chopped parsley

1. Beat cream cheese until smooth then work in blue cheese, Cheddar, nuts, cayenne pepper and garlic if used.

2. Shape into a large ball and roll in parsley, making sure it forms a thickish coating.

3. Stand on a serving plate and refrigerate 2 hours or until firm. Serve as a spread with the cream crackers.

Baby Footballs

Makes 30

Make as above, but roll mixture into 30 balls and coat with parsley. Put a cocktail stick into each and refrigerate 1 hour before serving. Alternatively, omit cocktail sticks and stand each ball on a small buttered biscuit, covered with a slice of ham cut to fit.

Fried Sausage 'Dumplings'

Makes 16

Simply made party snacks, ideal with hot punch and sparkling cider.

8 oz (225 g) pork sausage meat
2 oz (50 g) cashews, lightly toasted, fairly finely chopped
1 level tblsp finely chopped parsley
1 Grade 2 egg
2 tsp milk
1½ oz (40 g) fine dry breadcrumbs, lightly toasted
½ level tsp salt
½ level tsp onion or garlic salt
½ level tsp paprika
deep fat or oil for frying

1. Knead together sausage meat, cashews and parsley. With damp hands, shape into 16 miniature dumplings.

2. Coat in egg, well-beaten with the milk.

3. On a sheet of greaseproof paper or piece of foil, mix together the crumbs, salt, onion or garlic salt and paprika.

4. Add dumplings and coat all over with breadcrumb mixture. Leave to stand ½ hour for coating to settle.

5. Fry in deep hot fat or oil until golden brown and crisp. Remove from pan and drain on crumpled kitchen paper.

6. Spear a cocktail stick into each and serve hot.

Prune Roll-Ups
Makes 24

An ideal drinks party nibble, these are very easy to make and can be prepared ahead of time, left in the refrigerator and grilled just before eating.

24 stoned prunes, well-washed
cold tea or cider
24 blanched whole almonds
12 rashers of streaky bacon, de-rinded if necessary and halved

1. Soak prunes in a mixture of cold tea or cider until they soften and look fleshy and plump.

2. Drain thoroughly. Put a whole almond into each then wrap round with half a bacon rasher.

3. Secure bacon with cocktail sticks then grill until bacon crispens, turning once.

4. Drain on crumpled kitchen paper then transfer to a d'oyley-lined plate. Serve straight away.

Cheese Fondue and Brazil Nut Dip
Serves about 8

A rather unusual hot dip to serve with small, plain, unsweetened biscuits.

2 oz (50 g) butter or margarine
8 oz (125 g) any processed cheese, cut into very thin strips
1 garlic clove, peeled and crushed
3 drops Tabasco
4 tblsp dry cider
2 level tsp cornflour
3 tsp cold water
2 oz (50 g) brazil nuts, fairly finely chopped

1. Melt fat and cheese together over low heat. Stir in garlic, Tabasco, cider and cornflour mixed with cold water.

2. Heat until mixture just begins to bubble. Stir in nuts and transfer to bowl. Serve hot with dunks of small biscuits.

Crunchy Peanut Dip
Serves about 8

A super dip for small chipolata sausages and large, peeled prawns.

1 carton (5 oz or 142 ml) soured cream
4 oz (125 g) salted peanuts, finely chopped
2 oz (50 g) celery, scrubbed, dried, very finely chopped
2 rounded tblsp yogurt
2 level tblsp tomato purée
1 garlic clove, peeled and crushed or 2 oz (50 g) peeled and grated onion
salt and pepper to taste

1. Tip cream into a basin and mix in peanuts and celery. Thin down with yogurt and the purée.

2. Add garlic or onion and salt and pepper to taste. Spoon into a small dish, stand on a large plate and surround with hot sausages or prawns.

Aubergine Scoop
Serves 6 to 8

Although there is a certain kinship between this Middle Eastern-style aubergine mix and Mexican Quacamole based on avocados, I find this recipe somehow softer and gentler, at its most delicious scooped up with torn pieces of warm pitta bread. The technique of boiling aubergines came to me from the southern states of the USA and you will need a blender or food processor for successful results.

2 lb (900 g) aubergines
1 pt (575 ml) boiling water
1½ level tsp salt
3 oz (75 g) onion, peeled and finely grated
4 tblsp salad oil
3 to 4 tblsp mild vinegar
3 shakes Tabasco
3 medium blanched tomatoes, skinned, de-seeded, very finely
chopped
1 garlic clove, peeled and crushed
2 level tsp chopped mint
2 oz (50 g) walnuts, fairly finely chopped
seasoning to taste
3 rounded tblsp fresh chopped parsley or coriander

1. Peel and cut aubergines into large cubes. Cook in
   boiling, salted water for about ¼ hour, keeping pan
   covered.

2. Meanwhile, fry onion in the oil very gently. It should
   barely change colour — just soften slightly.

3. Drain aubergines thoroughly. Work to a purée in
   blender or food processor. Tip into a bowl. Add fried
   onions and any leftover oil then beat vinegar to taste.

4. Mix in Tabasco, tomatoes, garlic, mint, walnuts,
   sufficient salt and white pepper to suit personal taste,
   and half the parsley or coriander.

5. Spoon into a dish, sprinkle rest of parsley or coriander
   on top and serve as suggested in the introduction.

Soured Cream and Walnut Dip
Serves about 12

A classic style dip with which you can serve crudités of
mange tout, fingers of fresh pineapple, courgettes cut
into sticks, slices of peeled carrots and apple slices
brushed with lemon juice.

2 cartons (each 5 oz or 142 ml) soured cream
2 tblsp thick mayonnaise
1 level tblsp very finely grated onion
2 level tblsp very finely chopped parsley
1 oz (25 g) walnuts, very finely chopped
salt and freshly milled pepper to taste

1. Mix all ingredients well together and spoon into a
   small serving dish.

2. Stand on a large plate and surround with suggested
   crudités.

Flaming Igloo
Serves 8

Attractive on any table, this egg 'pâté' is best eaten with
fingers of hot toast or spread on to savoury biscuits.

8 Grade 1 or 2 eggs
2 oz (50 g) onion, peeled and grated
2 oz (50 g) blanched almonds, lightly toasted, fairly finely
chopped
thick mayonnaise (not salad cream)
seasoning to taste
4 oz (125 g) carrots, peeled and grated

1. Hardboil eggs. Shell when cold and grate directly into
   a bowl. Stir in onion, almonds and sufficient
   mayonnaise to bind mixture together.

2. Season to taste then mound into an igloo shape on a
   serving plate. Shower with grated carrots.

Nut Stuffed Eggs

Makes 16 halves

Finger food at its best.

8 Grade 1 or 2 eggs
2 rounded tblsp thick mayonnaise
1 rounded tblsp soured cream
2 tsp lemon juice
1 level tsp prepared mustard
1½ oz (40 g) hazelnuts, finely chopped
1 small can (about 3½ oz or 90 g) tuna, drained and finely mashed

Garnish
peeled onion slices separated into rings
bright orange lumpfish 'caviar' (sold in jars and often called mock caviar)
or 16 black olives
lettuce, finely shredded

1. Hardboil eggs then shell and halve lengthwise. Carefully remove yolks and put into bowl.

2. Mash finely then mix in mayonnaise, soured cream, lemon juice, mustard, hazelnuts and mashed tuna.

3. Mound smoothly into egg white halves then garnish each with 1 or 2 onion rings and either the orange lumpfish caviar or olives. Arrange on a lettuce-lined plate.

Liver Sausage Nut Diamonds

Makes about 26 to 30

Another delicious snack for any time of year. Serve the Diamonds straight from the oven with cups of hot coffee or keep them for drinks parties, especially those that run from morning till night during the Christmas festivities!

8 oz (225 g) plain flour
½ level tsp salt
½ level tsp powder mustard
4½ oz (140 g) butter or margarine
1 egg yolk
3 tblsp cold water
4 oz (125 g) fairly soft liver sausage
2 oz (50 g) flaked almonds, lightly toasted
egg white for brushing
poppy or sesame seeds

1. Sift flour, salt and mustard into bowl. Rub in butter or margarine finely. Using a fork, mix to a fairly stiff pastry with egg yolk and water.

2. Divide into 2 pieces and roll each into a 9 by 10 inch (22.5 by 25 cm) rectangle.

3. Place one rectangle on to a lightly greased baking tray. Spread with sausage, taking it right to edges. Sprinkle evenly with almonds.

4. Cover with second portion of pastry and press down lightly with a rolling pin.

5. Brush with lightly beaten egg white then dust with the poppy or sesame seeds. Bake 20 minutes in moderately hot oven, 400° F (200° C), Gas 6.

6. Cut into diamonds, remove from tray and arrange on a plate lined with a d'oyley or paper serviette.

Quiche Nut Tarts
Makes 18

A change from Mama and Papa Quiche, these smaller ones make tempting little snacks which are hard to refuse.

8 oz (225 g) plain flour
1 level tsp salt
4 oz (125 g) butter or margarine
½ oz (15 g) white cooking fat (vegetable) or lard if preferred
1 oz (25 g) salted peanuts, finely chopped
3½ to 4 tblsp cold water to mix

Filling
1 oz (25g) Gruyère cheese, finely grated
1 oz (25 g) walnuts, finely chopped
½ level tsp onion or garlic salt
¼ pt (150 ml) single cream
2 Grade 3 eggs
salt and pepper to taste
paprika

1. For pastry, sift flour and salt into bowl. Rub in butter or margarine and cooking fat or lard finely. Toss in peanuts.

2. Using a fork, mix to a stiffish pastry with water. Roll out thinly and cut into 18 rounds with a 3 inch (7.5 cm) cutter. Use to line 18 bun tins.

3. Mix together cheese, walnuts and either the onion or garlic salt. Spoon equal amounts into pastry cases.

4. Beat cream with eggs. Season to taste and pour over nut mixture filling each case equally. Dust with paprika.

5. Bake until golden and puffy, allowing 15 to 20 minutes in moderately hot oven, 375° F (190° C), Gas 5. Serve hot or warm.

Stuffed Mushrooms
Makes 36

Popular mushrooms form the basis of this fairly simple appetiser.

36 cap mushrooms, rinsed and patted dry, stalks removed
2 oz (50 g) butter or margarine
2 oz (50 g) green pepper, de-seeded and finely chopped
2 oz (50 g) onion, peeled and finely chopped
3 oz (75 g) fresh brown breadcrumbs
1½ oz (40 g) walnuts or pecans, finely chopped
½ level tsp salt
1 level tsp mixed herbs
½ level tsp ground ginger
1 tsp Worcester sauce
1 oz (25 g) extra melted butter or margarine

1. Arrange mushrooms on large, greased baking tray. Set oven to moderate, 350° F (180 ° C), Gas 4.

2. Chop mushroom stalks finely and leave aside for time being. Heat butter or margarine in pan. Add green pepper and onion. Fry gently until soft and just beginning to turn golden brown.

3. Stir in chopped mushroom stalks, crumbs, nuts, salt, herbs, ginger and Worcester sauce. Mix thoroughly then spoon equal amounts on to mushrooms.

4. Trickle a trace of melted butter or margarine over each then bake ¼ hour. Place under a hot grill until tops crispen, allowing about 3 minutes.

5. Transfer to a warm dish, put a cocktail stick into each and serve straight away.

Mushroom Walnut Tartlets
Makes 12

Savoury, wholesome, interesting and an ideal hot snack for a buffet party.

4 oz (125 g) plain flour
¼ level tsp salt
2 oz (50 g) butter or margarine
1 oz (25 g) walnuts, finely ground in blender or food processor
1 oz (25 g) stale Cheddar cheese, very finely grated
about 8 tsp cold water to mix

Filling
2 oz (50 g) mushrooms, trimmed, rinsed briefly, drained or patted dry
½ oz (15 g) butter or margarine
½ oz (15 g) plain flour
¼ pt (150 ml) single cream
½ level tsp salt
pepper to taste
1 level tblsp chopped fresh dill or parsley
12 freshly grilled button mushrooms

1. For pastry, sift flour and salt into a bowl. Rub in butter or margarine finely. Toss in nuts and cheese. Using a fork, stir to a fairly stiff pastry with water.

2. Roll out fairly thinly on floured surface. Cut into 12 rounds with a 2½ inch (about 6.25 cm) biscuit cutter, re-rolling and re-cutting trimmings to make the correct amount. Use to line 12 bun tins.

3. Press a square of foil into each and bake 7 minutes in oven set to hot, 425° F (220° C), Gas 7. Take out foil and continue to bake until pastry is golden brown; 5 to 7 minutes.

4. Meanwhile make sauce. Fry mushrooms faily briskly in the fat for about 3 minutes. Stir in flour to form a roux. Cook 1 more minute. Gradually blend in cream. Bring to boil, stirring continuously.

5. Season with salt and pepper to taste. Spoon into hot tartlet cases, sprinkle with dill or parsley, top each with a grilled mushroom and serve straight away.

SOUPS

Courgette Carrot Ripple Soup with Coconut

Serves 6 to 8

Different from run-of-the-mill soups, this one is delicately flavoured, not too rich, rippled with carrot purée (I use baby food) and topped with a sprinkling of toasted coconut.

2 lb (900 g) courgettes
1½ oz (40 g) butter or margarine
2 oz (50 g) onion, peeled and finely grated
1 pt (575 ml) stock
½ pt (275 ml) milk
1 to 2 level tsp salt
1½ level tblsp cornflour
3 tblsp cold water
4 level tblsp carrot purée
6 to 8 level tsp desiccated coconut, lightly toasted under the grill

1. Top and tail courgettes. Wash and dry, leave unpeeled and cut into very thin slices.

2. Heat butter or margarine in saucepan. Add onion and fry gently until soft but still very pale in colour.

3. Add courgettes, and mix with onions. Cover pan and fry slowly for 10 minutes. Stir from time to time.

4. Pour in stock and milk. Add salt. Bring to boil, lower heat and cover. Simmer over low heat for 20 minutes.

5. Blend to a smooth purée, in about 4 batches, in blender or food processor. Return to pan. Add cornflour mixed with the water.

6. Cook gently until soup comes to the boil and thickens. Simmer 5 minutes. Ladle into bowls and ripple in the heated carrot purée. Sprinkle each serving with coconut.

Pumpkin Soup

Serves 6 to 8

We make too little of pumpkin in this country, yet its cheerful orange colour adds a note of brightness to murky winter days. It readily replaces summer marrow and courgettes and is delicious when converted into the soup below. Use either imported canned pumpkin or, for economy, make your own by boiling peeled and diced pumkin until tender and working it to a purée in a blender or food processor.

1 oz (25 g) butter or margarine
3 oz (75 g) onion, peeled and very finely grated
1 can (14 oz or 400 g) pumpkin purée or the equivalent weight of homemade purée
1 pt (575 ml) milk
½ pt (275 ml) chicken stock or water
1 level tblsp cornflour
2 tblsp cold water
1 to 2 level tsp salt
2 oz (50 g) brazil nuts, very thinly sliced

1. Heat butter or margarine in a saucepan. Add onion and fry very gently over a low heat until soft but still pale in colour. Do not allow to brown.

2. Stir in pumpkin purée, milk and stock or water. Bring to boil, lower heat and cover. Simmer very gently for 7 minutes.

3. Mix cornflour smoothly with water. Add to soup. Heat gently, stirring, until it comes to boil and thickens. Season to taste with salt. Stir in half the brazils and ladle soup into warm bowls. Sprinkle rest of brazils on top of each serving.

Old-Fashioned Almond Soup
Serves 6

Nostalgically Victorian, this is a mild and genteel soup for entertaining special friends. Try to make this one with well-flavoured turkey or beef stock in preference to cubes and water.

1 oz (25 g) butter or margarine
2 oz (50 g) ground almonds
1 oz (25 g) plain flour
1 pt (575 ml) boiling stock
½ pt (275 ml) warm milk
½ level tsp salt
½ level tsp onion salt
white pepper to taste
1 oz (25 g) flaked almonds, lightly toasted

1. Melt butter or margarine in saucepan. Stir in ground almonds and fry over medium heat for about 5 to 8 minutes or until they turn a pale biscuity colour.

2. Add flour and cook a further minute, stirring continuously. Gradually blend in boiling stock, followed by milk.

3. When soup bubbles and has obviously thickened, season with both salts and pepper to taste. Stir frequently.

4. Ladle into 6 bowls or plates and sprinkle each with flaked almonds.

Chinese-Style Corn and Chicken Soup with Cashews
Serves 6 to 8

Appetising and fairly delicate, a pleasing prelude to a Chinese meal.

2 oz (50 g) butter or margarine
2 oz (50 g) plain flour
1¾ pt (1 litre) well-flavoured hot chicken or vegetable stock
(use 3 or 4 cubes in the absence of the real thing)
4 oz (125 g) cold cooked chicken, cut into strips
8 oz (225 g) frozen sweetcorn, used from frozen
2 oz (50 g) frozen peas, used from frozen
2 oz (50 g) cashews, lightly toasted, coarsely chopped
1 tsp soy sauce
salt and pepper to taste
a one-egg omelette, cut into strips.

1. Sizzle butter or margarine in a saucepan. Stir in flour to form a roux.

2. Gradually blend in hot stock, stirring smoothly until soup comes smoothly to the boil and thickens.

3. Stir in chicken, sweetcorn, peas, cashews, soy sauce and seasoning to taste. Bring to the boil again. Cover. Simmer for about 7 to 8 minutes or until piping hot.

4. Ladle into soup bowls or dishes and sprinkle each with omelette strips.

Sherry and Chestnut Soup
Serves 6

In the luxury bracket, keep this soup for special or festive occasions and sprinkle each serving with tiny bread croûtons, made by cutting white or brown bread into small cubes and frying them in oil, margarine or butter until golden brown. If you like the taste of garlic, add a peeled and sliced clove to the fat or oil while frying the bread.

1 oz (25 g) butter or margarine
1 oz (25 g) plain flour
1 pt (575 ml) well-flavoured hot chicken stock (use 2 cubes in the absence of the real thing)
1 can (15½ oz or 439 g) whole chestnuts in water (I used Clément Faugier brand)
½ level tsp salt
2 tblsp medium sherry
6 rounded tblsp croûtons

1. Heat butter or margarine in a saucepan. Stir in flour to form a roux. Cook 1 minute without browning.

2. Gradually blend in hot stock, stirring continuously until soup comes smoothly to the boil and thickens. Leave over a low heat.

3. Tip chestnuts and water into a bowl. Coarsely break up chestnuts with a fork

4. Add to soup with salt. Re-boil. Stir in sherry. Ladle into bowls or plates and add a tablespoon of croûtons to each.

Chilled Artichoke and Pine Nut Soup
Serves 6 to 8

Somewhat exotic, certainly luxurious and designed for lazy summer evenings, eating out on the patio or in the garden.

¾ pt (425 ml) chicken stock
½ pt (275 ml) cold milk
3 level tblsp instant mashed potato powder or rounded tblsp of potato granules
6 canned artichoke hearts, well-drained and each cut into quarters
½ level tsp onion powder
2 oz (50 g) pine nuts, lightly toasted
¼ pt (150 ml) double cream
salt and white pepper to taste

Garnish
a mixture of:
2 level tblsp chopped parsley
1 level tblsp chopped chives
1 level tsp finely chopped fresh mint

1. Pour stock and milk into a pan and bring to the boil. Gradually stir in potato powder and boil gently for 5 minutes.

2. Mix in artichoke hearts, onion powder, pine nuts and double cream. Season to taste, remove from heat and cool. Cover and refrigerate at least 4 hours.

3. Before serving, stir round and ladle into bowls. Sprinkle each with equal amounts of the herb mixture.

Fruit Consommé

Serves 6

Based on a mixture of two fruit juices, this is a glorious chilled soup-cum-jelly for hot days, and looks most elegant garnished with chopped green pistachio nuts or, for greater economy, walnuts. It is also very easy to make, perfect for a busy hostess.

1 pt (575 ml) mixture of apple and grape juice (use half of each)
2 level tsp gelatine
3 tblsp cold water
4 oz (125 g) green grapes, peeled, halved, pips removed
2 rounded tblsp chopped pistachio nuts or walnuts

1. Pour juice into bowl.

2. Tip gelatine into saucepan. Add water. Leave 5 minutes to soften. Stand over a low heat. Stir until melted and completely transparent.

3. Mix with the juice. Cover and refrigerate about 2 hours or until lightly set. Break up with a fork.

4. Divide grapes equally between 6 glass bowls. Top with equal amounts of the Fruit Consommé then sprinkle with the chopped pistachios or walnuts.

Tomato Consommé with Avocado Nut Sauce

Serves 6

A savoury version with a most unusual topping.

1 pt (575 ml) tomato juice
2 level tsp gelatine
3 tblsp cold water
1 level tsp celery salt
1 tsp Worcester sauce
1 medium ripe avocado
4 tblsp single cream
1 tblsp lemon juice
1 oz (25 g) walnuts, very finely chopped
seasoning to taste
2 level tsp finely grated orange peel

1. Pour juice into bowl.

2. Tip gelatine into saucepan. Add water. Leave 5 minutes to soften. Stand over a low heat. Stir until melted and completely transparent.

3. Mix with the juice and stir in celery salt and Worcester sauce. Cover and refrigerate about 2 hours or until lightly set. Break up with a fork.

4. Spoon into 6 glass bowls. For the Avocado Nut Sauce, halve avocado and mash flesh finely with cream and lemon juice. Stir in walnuts.

5. Season to taste then spoon over Consommé. Sprinkle with orange peel and serve.

Chilled Cucumber Yogurt Soup with Walnuts
Serves 6

From hotter climes comes this Balkan-style soup which is enjoyed with equal enthusiasm in the Middle East.

1 large cucumber, peeled
10 oz (275 g) natural yogurt
2 oz (50 g) walnuts, very finely chopped
1 garlic clove, peeled and crushed
2 tblsp fresh, strained lemon juice
½ pt (275 ml) milk
1 level tsp finely chopped fresh mint (optional)
2 to 3 level tsp salt

Garnish
3 level tblsp chopped parsley, dill or fresh coriander

1. Pare cucumber into thin slices on side of grater. Tip into a tea towel and wring as dry as possible.

2. In separate bowl, beat together the yogurt, walnuts, garlic, lemon juice, milk, mint and salt. Stir in cucumber thoroughly.

3. Cover and refrigerate at least 3 hours. Stir round before serving, ladle into soup bowls and sprinkle each with either parsley, dill or the coriander.

Chilled Asparagus 'Broth'
Serves 6

Cool and cucumber-fresh, a delightful soup for hot days and very easy to make.

1 can condensed asparagus soup
½ pt (275 ml) water
1 carton (5 oz or 142 ml) soured cream
¼ large cucumber, peeled, grated, wrung dry in tea towel
1 bunch spring onions, trimmed, washed, very finely chopped
1 oz (25 g) green pepper, very finely chopped
milk or yogurt if necessary
3 rounded tblsp walnuts, finely chopped
3 level tblsp chopped celery

1. Spoon asparagus soup into bowl then smoothly whisk in water and soured cream.

2. Stir in cucumber, onions and green pepper, thinning down with milk or yogurt if soup is too thick for personal taste.

3. Cover and refrigerate at least 3 hours. Stir round before serving, ladle into bowls and sprinkle with equal amounts of walnuts and celery.

STARTERS

Firelight Cocktail
Serves 8

A very pretty starter, glowing with colour and light enough to be followed by a substantial meal.

8 heaped tblsp finely shredded crisp lettuce
1 can (about 15 oz or 425 g) apricot halves
1 lb (450 g) blanched tomatoes, skinned
1 bunch spring onions
1 level tblsp chopped chives
1 level tblsp chopped parsley
1 oz (25 g) salted cashews
1 oz (25 g) salted peanuts
1 oz (25 g) salted almonds, coarsely chopped
4 tblsp well-flavoured French dressing
½ level tsp tarragon
mustard and cress

1. Divide lettuce equally between 8 wine glasses with short stems.

2. Drain apricots thoroughly and cut each half into 4 pieces. Reserve syrup or juice for drinks, etc.

3. Transfer apricots to a mixing bowl. Cut each tomato into eighths. Trim spring onions then chop into short lengths. Add tomatoes and onions to apricots in bowl.

4. Gently mix in chives, parsley and all 3 varieties of nuts. Coat with salad dressing, whisked with the tarragon.

5. Toss with 2 spoons then transfer equal amounts to the glasses. Shower with washed mustard and cress.

Kiwi Fruit and Melon Cocktail
Serves 6

Golden green, highlighted by even greener pistachios and a zippy dressing choc-a-bloc with chopped parsley and chives. Cooling on a summer's day.

4 kiwi fruits
1 medium ripe melon
¼ medium cucumber, washed, dried, left unpeeled
½ oz (15 g) pistachio nuts, blanched, skinned, chopped or taken out of shells if roasted and also finely chopped
2 rounded tblsp chopped parsley
1 rounded tblsp chopped chives
4 tblsp well-flavoured French dressing
8 orange slices, unpeeled, each slit from centre to outside edge

1. Peel kiwi fruit and thinly slice. Tip into a bowl.

2. Halve melon, remove and discard seeds and scoop flesh directly into bowl of kiwis, using either a melon baller or teaspoon.

3. Cut cucumber into tiny dice and add to both fruits with the pistachio nuts.

4. Transfer to 6 wine-type glasses. Beat parsley and chives into dressing then pour equal amounts over fruit, etc.

5. Decorate each with a slice of orange, shaped into a twist.

Prawn Pears with Walnut Cream Sauce

Serves 4

A variation on the prawn cocktail theme. Unusual and very much the thing for a small dinner party.

lettuce leaves, washed, drained, patted dry
8 canned pear halves, well-drained
8 oz (225 g) peeled prawns, thawed if frozen
1 carton (5 oz or 142 ml) soured cream
1 tblsp milk
1 oz (25 g) walnuts, very finely chopped
salt and pepper to taste
8 unpeeled prawns or 8 cucumber slices, unpeeled

1. Line 4 small plates with lettuce leaves. Arrange 2 pear halves, cut side uppermost, on top of each

2. Fill hollows with prawns. For sauce, beat soured cream with milk. Stir in walnuts. Season to taste with salt and pepper.

3. Spoon over prawns. Decorate each with a whole prawn or slice of cucumber, first slit from centre to outside edge and shaped into a twist.

Noodles with Pesto

Serves 6

Pesto is an imaginative Italian sauce from Genoa, perfumed with basil and nuts. It has no rival in the sauce repetoire and is a joy mixed with any kind of pasta. In Italy, it is also stirred into Minestrone to intensify the flavour of the soup. Pesto should be made entirely from basil but as this herb does not grow as profusely here as it does in southern Europe, I have compromised and used half garden-grown basil and half parsley. As the sauce is fairly pungent, it should be used sparingly and half the amount serves 6.

1 oz (25 g) basil leaves
1 oz (25 g) parsley, minus stalks
1 oz (25 g) pine nuts or walnuts
1 oz (25 g) soft butter
3 oz (75 g) Parmesan cheese, cubed
3 tblsp light olive oil or corn oil if preferred
1 garlic clove, peeled
2 tblsp boiling water
salt to taste
1 lb (450 g) freshly cooked flat noodles

1. Tip first 7 ingredients into a blender goblet or food processor. Run machine until ingredients form a paste.

2. Spoon into a bowl and beat in boiling water. Season to taste with salt.

3. Use half with the noodles. Spoon remainder into a small pot or jar, cover with oil (as it forms an almost airtight seal) then overwrap with cling film. Store up to 2 months in the refrigerator.

Pistachio Liver Paste

Serves 6

Quick and easy, this is nevertheless a luxury-style liver paste tinged with alcohol and mixed with costly pistachio nuts and black olives. Serve it with fingers of hot toast.

12 oz (350 g) soft liver sausage (Belgian, French or German)
2 oz (50 g) butter, at kitchen temperature, softened
1 oz (25 g) pistachio nuts, blanched, skinned, finely chopped (if bought in split shells and aready roasted, allow 2 to 3 oz or 50 to 75 g)
1 rounded tblsp finely chopped black olives
2 tsp Grand Marnier

1. Beat liver sausage smoothly with butter.

2. Stir in nuts, olives and the liqueur. Spoon into a small dish.

3. Cover and refrigerate 1 to 2 hours or until firm. Spoon portions out on to plates and pass round hot toast.

Chef's Hors d'Oeuvre Salad Bowls
Serves 4

Although I first tasted this in North America, I had something similar recently in a very classy French restaurant in London's Knightsbridge. It is obviously catching on as an appealing meal starter.

4 oz (126 g) spinach, thoroughly washed, dried, shredded
6 oz (175 g) streaky bacon, chopped, fried until crisp in its own fat
2 slices white or brown bread, cut into tiny cubes, fried until golden in butter or margarine
3 oz (75 g) brazil nuts, cut into very thin slivers
8 oz (225 g) cottage cheese
1 bunch spring onions, trimmed, chopped
French dressing to moisten
1 head of chicory, leaves separated out, washed, dried
2 hardboiled egg yolks

1. Put spinach into large bowl. Add bacon, fried bread cubes, nuts, cottage cheese and onions.

2. Toss with sufficient mild French dressing to moisten.

3. Spoon into 4 bowls, each lined with chicory leaves to resemble petals of a flower.

4. Rub egg yolks through a sieve directly over the top of each salad.

Antipasto Romana
Serves 6

Popular in restaurants both here and in Italy, this multi-coloured starter is easy to copy and, with its walnut dressing, has style and chic.

8 oz (225 g) Mozzerella cheese
1 lb (450 g) blanched tomatoes, skinned, thinly sliced
1 large avocado, peeled, halved, flesh cut into long slices, sprinkled with lemon juice
4 oz (125 g) onion, peeled, thinly sliced, slices separated into rings
2 oz (50 g) small black olives
4 tblsp olive oil (or use half walnut oil and half corn)
1 level tsp salt
1 level tsp caster sugar
1 level tsp powder mustard
1 garlic clove, peeled and crushed (optional)
1 tblsp lemon juice
1 tblsp wine vinegar
1½ oz (40 g) walnuts, very finely chopped or even ground
curly endive, well-washed to remove grit, well-drained

1. Thinly slice cheese. Arrange on 6 individual plates alternately with tomato slices.

2. Top with slices of avocado, onion rings and the olives.

3. To make dressing, beat oil with salt, sugar, mustard and garlic if used. Beat in lemon juice, vinegar and walnuts.

4. Spoon over salad then garnish each with a fringe of curly endive.

Lancashire Cheese and Nut Puffs
Serves 4

A rich starter made with rounds of bread fried in garlic butter and topped with soft cheese, nuts and egg. It is on the filling side, so follow with a light main course and sweet based on fruit.

8 slices white or brown bread
3 oz (75 g) butter
2 tsp salad oil
1 garlic clove, peeled and crushed
4 oz (125 g) Lancashire cheese, crumbled or grated
2 oz (50 g) full-fat cream cheese
1 oz (25 g) walnuts, finely chopped
1 Grade 2 egg, separated
seasoning to taste
2 or 3 drops of lemon juice
1 oz (25 g) flaked almonds

1. Cut bread into rounds with a 2½ to 3 inch (6.25 to 7.5 cm) biscuit cutter. (Keep edges for crumbs.)

2. Heat 2 oz (50 g) butter, oil and garlic in frying pan. Add bread, 2 or 3 rounds at a time, and fry until golden brown and crisp on both sides. Drain.

3. Soften remaining butter then beat until smooth with both cheeses, walnuts and egg yolk. Season to taste with salt and pepper.

4. Beat egg white and lemon juice to a stiff snow. Gently fold into cheese mixture.

5. Spread over fried bread rounds, sprinkle with almonds and grill until topping puffs up and the nuts turn golden brown. Serve straight away, allowing 2 per person.

Swiss Cheese Puffs
Serves 4

Feather-light and warm golden brown, these little Cheese Puffs are a cross between a soufflé and bread pudding.

2 Grade 2 eggs
½ pt (275 ml) single cream, heated to lukewarm
2 oz (50 g) soft white breadcrumbs, made from fresh bread
3 oz (75 g) Gruyère or Emmental cheese, very finely grated
1 oz (25 g) blanched almonds, skinned, lightly toasted, finely chopped
½ level tsp prepared English mustard
½ level tsp salt
3 drops lemon juice
watercress

1. Separate eggs, dropping yolks into one bowl and whites into another.

2. Beat warm cream into egg yolks then stir in crumbs, cheese, almonds, mustard and salt. Mix well. Cover. Leave to stand ½ hour.

3. Whip egg whites and lemon juice to a stiff snow. Fold into the cheese and breadcrumb mixture. When smooth and evenly combined, transfer to 4 individual heatproof dishes, first well-greased.

4. Bake 20 to 30 minutes in moderately hot oven, 400° F (200° C), Gas 6. Remove from oven, garnish with watercress and serve straight away.

Avocado with Walnut Dressing
Serves 4

A sharpish, Italian-style dressing is a zesty foil for this bland and creamy fruit, filled with light and dark crabmeat.

4 tblsp olive or other salad oil to taste
4 canned anchovies in oil, drained, finely chopped or 1 tsp anchovy essence
1 garlic clove, peeled and crushed
1 oz (25 g) walnuts, very finely chopped
1 level tsp prepared Continental mustard
1 rounded tblsp very finely chopped parsley
1 level tsp finely chopped capers
½ level tsp finely chopped fresh mint
1 tblsp lemon juice
1 tblsp wine or cider vinegar
2 large, ripe avocados
extra lemon juice
6 oz (175 g) light and dark crabmeat, fresh or canned
4 lettuce-lined plates

1. Pour oil into a small bowl. Add anchovies or anchovy essence, garlic, walnuts, mustard, parsley, capers and mint. Beat in lemon juice and vinegar.

2. Halve avocados, remove stones and brush flesh with lemon juice to prevent browning. Mix light and dark crabmeat together and spoon into avocado halves.

3. Stand on lettuce-lined plates and coat heavily with the prepared dressing, beaten again just before using.

Bacon and Almond Avocados
Serves 4

Blessed with a sumptuous filling, these are a far cry from avocados with a simple French dressing!

4 oz (125 g) unsmoked streaky bacon, finely chopped
2 Grade 3 hardboiled eggs, shelled, grated into a bowl
8 medium spring onions, trimmed, finely chopped
2 oz (50 g) blanched almonds, skinned, toasted, chopped
1 rounded tblsp stuffed olives, chopped
seasoning to taste
2 to 3 tblsp mayonnaise
2 large ripe avocados, halved, stones removed
Worcester sauce
lemon juice
strips of red pepper for garnishing

1. Fry bacon in its own fat until crisp and golden brown. Remove from pan and drain on kitchen paper.

2. Transfer to bowl. Mix in eggs, onions, almonds and olives. Season. Add sufficient mayonnaise to bind mixture together.

3. Halve avocados and pour ½ tsp Worcester sauce into each hollow. Brush flesh all over with lemon juice to prevent discolouration.

4. Pile egg mixture into each half then garnish.

Salmon and Hazelnut Mousse Bowls

Serves 6

Made from canned salmon and port, the result is quite impressive, worth keeping for special occasions.

1 can (7 oz or about 200 g) red salmon
1 level tblsp thick mayonnaise
1 level tsp prepared mustard (English)
1 Grade 2 egg, separated
1 envelope gelatine
¼ pt (150 ml) cold water
3 tblsp port
1 level tsp onion salt
salt and pepper to taste
¼ tsp lemon juice
¼ pt (150 ml) double cream

Topping
6 heaped tsp thick mayonnaise
1 oz (25 g) hazelnuts, very finely chopped
6 lemon wedges
3 large black grapes, halved and de-seeded

1. Tip salmon and liquid into a basin. Remove bones and any dark skin then finely mash flesh. Beat in mayonnaise, mustard and egg yolk. Alternatively, work these ingredients smoothly together in blender or food processor.

2. Soften gelatine in cold water for 5 minutes then melt gently over low heat in small pan. Stir in port then blend smoothly with salmon mixture. Season with onion salt, ordinary salt and pepper to taste. Leave in the cool until *just beginning* to thicken and set.

3. Beat egg whites to a stiff snow with lemon juice. Whip cream until thick. Using a large metal spoon or spatula, fold both alternately into salmon mixture.

4. When smooth and evenly-combined, transfer equal amounts to 6 glass dishes. Refrigerate until set. Before serving, top each with a teaspoon of mayonnaise and shower thickly with nuts. Garnish each with a lemon wedge and grape half.

Marinaded Mushrooms with Brazils

Serves 6

Raw mushrooms have a subtle, woodland flavour and make a distinctive starter when mixed with brazil nuts and marinated in a piquant dressing.

1 lb (450 g) button mushrooms, trimmed, washed, drained, thinly sliced
3 oz (75 g) brazil nuts, very thinly sliced
6 tblsp salad oil
1 garlic clove, peeled and crushed (optional)
2 oz (50 g) onion, peeled and grated
1 level tsp powder mustard
1 level tsp dried basil
1 tsp soy sauce
2 tblsp lemon juice
1 tblsp wine vinegar
salt and pepper to taste
mustard and cress

1. Tip mushrooms into a bowl and, with fingers, mix with the sliced brazils.

2. For dressing, beat oil with garlic clove (if used) onion, mustard, basil and soy sauce.

3. Whisk in lemon juice and vinegar then season to taste with salt and pepper.

4. Pour over mushrooms and toss gently with 2 spoons. Transfer to 6 serving bowls and sprinkle each thickly with mustard and cress.

Eastern-Style Rice Starter
Serves 6

Fruit, nuts, chicken, gammon and a slightly unusual dressing turn this easy rice dish into something quite special.

6 oz (175 g) easy-cook, long grain rice
12 fluid oz (325 ml) boiling water
1 level tsp salt
8 oz (225 g) cold cooked chicken, cut into tiny dice
4 oz (125 g) boiled gammon, cut into tiny dice
3 oz (75 g) onion, peeled and grated
1 large celery stalk, scrubbed and thinly sliced
1 can mandarin oranges, drained (keep syrup for drinks)
2 oz (50 g) whole blanched almonds, toasted, cut into spikes
1 small can evaporated milk
2 tsp salad oil
2 tblsp lemon juice
1 tblsp wine vinegar
1 to 1½ level tsp salt
white pepper to taste
1 lb (450 g) blanched tomatoes, skinned and thinly sliced
3 rounded tblsp unpeeled, diced cucumber

1. Cook rice in the boiling water and salt for 15 to 17 minutes or until grains are plump and tender and have absorbed all the liquid. Keep pan covered and leave rice undisturbed. Cool completely and tip into bowl.

2. Add chicken, gammon, onion, celery, two-thirds of the mandarins and half the almonds.

3. Beat milk with oil, lemon juice, vinegar, salt and pepper to taste. Pour over the rice mixture and toss well with 2 spoons.

4. Line 6 small plates with tomatoes then mound rice salad on top of each. Garnish with remaining mandarins, almonds and cucumber dice.

Christmas Turkey 'Brawn'
Serves 6

Always wondering what to do with left-over turkey, I found one solution which converts into this tasty starter. The novelty is in the topping of apple sauce dusted with cinnamon and a hint of nuts.

1 envelope gelatine
5 tblsp cold water
5 rounded tblsp mayonnaise
1 carton (5 oz or 142 g) soured cream
2 tblsp milk
1 tblsp tarragon vinegar
½ tsp Tabasco
3 oz (75 g) onion, peeled, grated
2 rounded tblsp chopped stuffed olives
2 rounded tblsp chopped gherkins
1 rounded tsp prepared English mustard
3 oz (75 g) pecan nuts or walnuts, finely chopped
8 oz (225 g) cold cooked turkey, cut into small dice
6 rounded tblsp apple sauce
cinnamon

1. Tip gelatine into a saucepan. Add water and leave 5 minutes to soften. Stand over a low heat and stir until dissolved.

2. Beat melted gelatine into mayonnaise. Add soured cream, milk, vinegar, Tabasco, onion, olives, gherkins and mustard.

3. Cover. Refrigerate until cold and just beginning to thicken and set.

4. Fold in two-thirds of the nuts and all the turkey. Spoon into 6 dishes and set in the refrigerator.

5. Before serving, spoon apple sauce on top of each then sprinkle with remaining nuts and cinnamon.

MAIN COURSES

Trout with Almonds
Serves 4

The classic trout dish, well-beloved with sauté potatoes, and a selection of cooked vegetables or a mixed salad.

4 medium trout, each about 12 oz or 350 g, gutted and scaled
4 level tblsp plain flour ⎱ *mixed*
1 level tsp salt ⎰
4 oz (125 g) butter or margarine (or mixture)
3 tsp salad oil
4 oz (125 g) flaked almonds
lemon slices and parsley for garnishing

1. Leave heads and tails on trout to prevent shrinkage. Wash and wipe dry. Coat with flour and salt mixture.

2. Heat 3 oz (75 g) butter or margarine and the salad oil in a large frying pan. Add trout, two at a time, and fry until cooked through and golden; 5 to 6 minutes per side. Turn twice.

3. Drain on crumpled kitchen paper. Repeat with remaining trout. Add last 1 oz (25 g) butter to pan. Add almonds and fry gently until golden.

4. Arrange trout on 4 warm plates. Coat each with hot butter or margarine mixture and the almonds. Garnish with lemon and parsley and serve straight away.

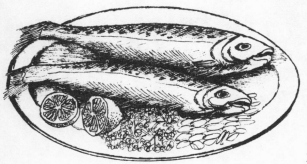

Coconut Cod Crisp
Serves 4

Cod in fancy dress, modest in its own way, most acceptable with sauté potatoes and a collection of cooked peas and carrots plus cauliflower in cheese sauce.

1½ lb (675 g) cod fillet, skinned, cut into 2 inch (5 cm) cubes
2 oz (50 g) butter or margarine
2 tsp salad oil
3 oz (75 g) fresh white breadcrumbs
1 oz (25 g) desiccated coconut
1 garlic clove, peeled and crushed
2 level tsp lemon peel
1 level tsp salt
5 tblsp pineapple juice
4 wedges of orange for garnish (peel left on)

1. Wash cod and pat dry. Heat butter or margarine and oil in a pan until sizzling.

2. Add crumbs, coconut and garlic. Fry over medium heat until ingredients turn a warm gold. Stir in lemon peel.

3. Put fish into a shallow, greased heatproof dish to form a single layer. Season with salt then moisten with pineapple juice.

4. Sprinkle with fried crumb mixture. Cook, uncovered, for 15 to 20 minutes in hot oven, 425° F (220° C), Gas 7. Garnish with orange wedges.

South Sea Island Cod Steaks
Serves 4

Cod with a difference, as you can see. Serve the fish with whole bananas fried in butter or margarine and mounds of creamed potatoes. A crunchy salad goes well with the fish and its accompaniments.

4 large cod steaks
cold water
3 lemon slices
1 small bay leaf
1 small onion, peeled and sliced
2 level tsp salt
1 carton (5 oz or 142 ml) soured cream
1 oz (25 g) melted butter or margarine
1 tblsp milk
16 canned peach slices, well-drained
4 level tblsp desiccated coconut

1. In large frying pan, arrange cod steaks in a single layer. Cover with water then add lemon slices, bay leaf and onion slices. Season with half the salt.

2. Bring water just up to the boil. Lower heat and cover. Poach very gently for ¼ hour.

3. Lift out of pan with a fish slice and drain thoroughly by standing on a clean tea towel.

4. Transfer to a buttered heatproof dish. Beat cream with butter or margarine, the milk and rest of salt.

5. Spoon over fish. Top each with 4 peach slices then sprinkle with coconut. Grill 3 to 5 minutes or until cream begins to bubble and coconut is crunchy and golden.

Smoked Haddock Provençale
Serves 4

In southern France, this would probably be made with dried cod, difficult to come by over here. Smoked haddock makes an admirable substitute for a characterful fish dish, a pleasure to eat with crusty French bread and butter.

1½ lb (675 g) smoked haddock fillet, skinned
cold water
3 tblsp salad oil
2 oz (50 g) walnuts, coarsely chopped
3 oz (75 g) onions, peeled and grated
1 level tblsp plain flour
12 oz (350 g) ripe tomatoes, blanched, skinned, chopped
2 level tsp brown sugar
1 rounded tsp fresh chopped basil or ½ level tsp dried
pepper to taste
chopped parsley

1. Cut haddock into 4 portions. Put into large frying pan and cover with cold water. Bring to boil and drain. Repeat once more to remove excess saltiness. Arrange, in single layer, in greased heatproof casserole dish.

2. Heat oil in a clean pan until hot and sizzling. Add walnuts and onions. Fry over medium heat until pale golden brown.

3. Stir in flour and cook an extra minute. Mix in tomatoes, sugar, basil and pepper to taste.

4. Spoon over fish in dish. Reheat, uncovered, for ¼ hour in hot oven, 425° F (220° C), Gas 7. Sprinkle thickly with parsley and serve.

Note
For an authentic touch, fry ingredients in olive oil, spoon over fish as given in previous recipe then stud with 2 oz (50 g) small black olives and 6 to 8 canned anchovy fillets.

Tuna and Cheese Casserole
Serves 4

An easy winner of a casserole. Try it with a salad of tomatoes, red peppers and sliced radishes, tossed in French dressing.

6 oz (175 g) green noodles
boiling salted water
2 oz (50 g) butter or margarine
2 oz (50 g) onion, peeled, chopped
1 oz (25 g) plain flour
½ pt (275 ml) warm milk
3 oz (75 g) sage Derby cheese, grated
1 can (7 oz or 200 g) tuna, drained, flaked
1 rounded tsp finely grated lemon peel
1 tblsp lemon juice
seasoning to taste
1 oz (25 g) ground almonds
2 rounded tblsp lightly toasted breadcrumbs

1. Cook noodles in boiling salted water for about 10 to 12 minutes or until tender but still firm. Drain.

2. Melt 1 oz (25 g) butter or margarine in a saucepan. Add onion and fry gently until soft but still pale in colour.

3. Stir in flour and cook a further ½ minute. Gradually blend in milk.

4. Cook over a low heat, stirring, until sauce bubbles and thickens. Mix in cheese. Continue to stir until melted.

5. Remove from heat. Add flaked tuna, lemon peel, lemon juice, drained noodles and seasoning to taste.

6. Transfer smoothly to a 1½ pint (1 litre) greased heatproof casserole dish. Sprinkle with almonds and breadcrumbs. Melt rest of butter or margarine and sprinkle over the top.

7. Reheat and brown for 15 minutes in hot oven, 425° F (220° C), Gas 7. Serve straight away.

Curry of Chicken
Serves 4 to 6

A fairly gentle curry with mixed fruits and coconut. Its obvious partner is rice and it also responds well to side dishes of yogurt, chutney, chopped-up onions sprinkled with paprika and mint jelly. It is an anglicised version of the real thing.

4 large chicken joints, each divided into 2 pieces
2 oz (50 g) butter or margarine
2 tsp salad oil
8 oz (225 g) onions, peeled, grated
1 garlic clove, peeled and crushed
1 oz (25 g) fresh ginger, peeled, chopped
4 oz (125 g) cooking apple, peeled, quartered, cored, chopped
2 oz (50 g) seedless raisins
2 level tblsp tubed or canned tomato purée
1½ oz (40 g) desiccated coconut
1 rounded tblsp mango chutney
1 to 3 level tsp curry powder, depending on personal taste
½ pt (275 ml) apple juice
1½ to 2 level tsp salt
1½ level tblsp cornflour

1. Wash and dry chicken. Heat butter or margarine and oil in a large pan. Add chicken and fry fairly briskly until crisp and golden, turning once. Remove to plate for time being.

2. Add onions and garlic to pan. Fry until golden. Stir in ginger, apple, raisins, tomato purée, coconut, chutney and curry powder. Stir in all but 3 tablespoons of apple juice.

3. Season with salt, replace chicken and bring to the boil. Lower heat and cover. Simmer ¾ hour, keeping heat gentle. Stir 3 or 4 times.

4. Mix cornflour smoothly with rest of apple juice. Add to curry mixture and boil gently until it thickens, stirring. Serve with suggested accompaniments.

Creamy Cider Chicken and Almonds
Serves 4

Simmered in cider and economically enriched with evaporated milk, this is chicken in the haute cuisine class without the usual price tag attached! Serve with rice and mixed vegetables.

4 chicken joints (2 lb or 900 g), skinned
3 level tblsp plain flour
2 oz (50 g) butter or margarine
2 tsp salad oil
4 oz (125 g) streaky bacon, chopped
4 oz (125 g) onions, peeled, grated
4 oz (125 g) carrots, peeled, grated
¾ pt (425 ml) medium cider
2 level tsp salt
4 oz (125 g) button mushrooms, washed, drained, left whole
2 oz (50 g) flaked almonds, toasted until light brown
1 small can evaporated milk
pepper to taste
3 heaped tblsp finely chopped parsley

1. Wash and dry chicken. Coat with flour, shaking off surplus. Heat butter or margarine and oil in large pan. Add chicken joints and fry briskly until golden, turning once.

2. Remove chicken to plate. Add bacon to pan with onions and carrots. Fry over medium heat until golden brown, tuning to prevent sticking.

3. Pour cider into pan then add salt. Bring to boil, replace chicken, lower heat and cover. Simmer ¾ hour or until chicken is just tender. Stir from time to time.

4. Mix in mushrooms, almonds, evaporated milk and pepper to taste. Leave uncovered and continue to simmer a further ¼ hour.

5. Transfer to 4 warm dinner plates and sprinkle heavily with parsley.

Chopstick Chicken
Serves 6 to 8

A Far Eastern-style chicken dish with a mild, elusive flavour. Serve with-rice, cooked bean sprouts and mange tout.

2 lb (900 g) boned chicken breasts (or use turkey if preferred), thawed if frozen
1 tblsp bland oil
8 oz (225 g) onions
3 oz (75 g) chunky peanut butter
1 garlic clove, peeled and crushed
¾ pt (425 ml) water
1 to 2 level tsp salt
2 level tsp mild curry powder
½ level tsp ground coriander
½ level tsp ground ginger
seeds from 4 opened-out cardamom pods
1 level tblsp cornflour, smoothly mixed with 2 tblsp cold water
2 oz (50 g) unsalted peanuts, lightly toasted, skins rubbed off, coarsely chopped
2 tomatoes, each cut into 8 wedges

1. Wash and dry chicken breasts. Cut into 1 by ½ inch (2.5 by 1.25 cm) wide strips

2. Heat oil in pan until hot and sizzling. Add onions and fry until golden. Mix in chicken strips and continue to fry until they turn from pink to almost white.

3. Mix in peanut butter, garlic, water, salt, curry powder, coriander, ground ginger and cardamom seeds. Bring to boil, stirring. Lower heat and cover pan.

4. Simmer 30 to 40 minutes or until chicken is tender. Stir in cornflour and water. Boil gently to thicken.

5. Spoon into a warm serving dish and sprinkle with peanuts. Garnish attractively with wedges of tomato.

Chicken in the Jungle
Serves 8

Sophisticated in flavour and appearance, this is a quickly-prepared chicken dish made from an exotic, but readily available, mix of ingredients. It cooks happily away in the oven, undemanding of time or attention, and also freezes well.

8 oz (225 g) easy-cook, long grain rice
1 pt (575 ml) boiling water
1 level tsp salt
6 oz (175 g) onions, peeled and chopped
6 oz (175 g) mixture of red and green peppers, cut into small cubes
extra water
1 small can of evaporated milk
2 oz (50 g) brazil nuts, very thinly sliced
3 lb (1½ kg) chicken legs and thighs
paprika

1. Put rice into a pan with water and salt. Stir round and bring to boil. Lower heat and cover. Cook, undisturbed, for ¼ hour or until rice grains are plump and tender and have absorbed all the water.

2. Boil onions and peppers for 3 minutes in enough extra water to cover. Drain. Fork into rice with the evaporated milk and nuts. Adjust seasoning to taste.

3. Spread over base of 10 by 8 inch (25 by 20 cm) oblong casserole dish. Top with chicken and sprinkle with paprika.

4. Leave uncovered and bake 1¼ hours in moderately hot oven, 375° F (190° C), Gas 5. Serve with spinach, freshly boiled green cabbage, sprouts or a large mixed salad.

Christmas Turkey with Tutti Frutti Almond Stuffing
Serves 12 to 14

I have used a deep-basted bird for this one and packed the neck cavity with a surprise stuffing of fruit and nuts, untraditional perhaps, but lively and finely-flavoured. One tip here that I believe is worth heeding. Keep the body cavity of the bird empty as the heat of the oven is rarely able to penetrate through to the centre of the stuffing or the surrounding turkey meat. As a result, bacteria develop and multiply, often causing stomach upsets and even food poisoning.

1 by 10 lb (5 kg) deep-basted turkey, thawed if frozen, giblet bag removed
6 oz (175 g) fresh white or brown breadcrumbs
1½ oz (40 g) seedless raisins
1 oz (25 g) cooking dates, chopped
1 oz (25 g) prunes, weight after stoning, washed, soaked overnight, chopped
2 oz (50 g) dried apricots, washed, soaked overnight, chopped
2 oz (30 g) blanched almonds, skinned, lightly toasted, chopped
1 level tsp salt
1 Grade 2 egg, beaten
2 tblsp medium sherry

1. Wash turkey inside and out under cold, running water. Wipe dry with kitchen paper. Set oven to moderate, 350° F (180° C), Gas 4.

2. For stuffing, tip crumbs into a bowl. Add fruit, almonds and salt. Bind with egg and sherry. Pack into neck end of turkey. Stand on rack in large roasting tin and brush with melted fat.

3. Roast 3 to 3½ hours or until juices run clear when thickest part of the thigh is punctured with a fine skewer.

4. If breast is darkening too much, cover with foil for the last ½ to ¾ hour of roasting.

5. Uncover and leave turkey to stand 10 to 15 minutes before carving as this gives flesh a chance to firm-up and stops the breast meat from crumbling.

Note
If using same stuffing for a chicken, halve all the amounts.

Wine-Braised Liver with Chestnuts
Serves 4

A hearty offal dish laced with wine and flavoured in a subtle way with chestnuts.

1 lb (450 g) pig's liver
cold milk
4 level tblsp plain flour
2 oz (50 g) butter or margarine
1 tsp salad oil
2 oz (50 g) celery, scrubbed, thinly sliced
4 oz (125 g) carrots, peeled, very thinly sliced
6 oz (175 g) onion, peeled, thinly sliced
6 oz (175 g) potato, peeled, washed, diced
½ pt (275 ml) dry red wine
¼ pt (150 ml) water
8 oz (225 g) cooked chestnuts (weight after peeling), broken into chunks
2 level tsp salt
1 level tsp thyme

1. Cube liver and soak for 2 hours in milk to cover to remove any bitterness. Pat dry and toss in flour.

2. Heat butter or margarine and oil in a pan. Add liver and fry briskly until well-sealed and golden. Remove from pan and leave aside for time being.

3. Add prepared vegetables to pan and fry until golden. Replace liver (with any left-over flour) then mix in wine, water and chestnuts.

4. Season to taste with salt and add thyme. Cook, stirring, until mixture comes to the boil.

5. Reduce heat and cover pan. Simmer about 35 to 40 minutes or until liver is tender, stirring from time to time to prevent sticking. Serve with boiled potatoes and assorted vegetables to taste.

Kidneys and Chestnuts on Skewers
Serves 4

Very popular with family and friends, this is an unusual way of presenting both kidneys and chestnuts.

8 lambs' kidneys
8 fairly long rashers of green streaky bacon
16 cooked chestnuts, as large as possible
1 oz (25 g) butter or margarine, melted
buttered rice for serving

1. Skin kidneys then cut in half and remove cores. Cut each half into 2 pieces.

2. Halve bacon rashers and wrap round chestnuts.

3. Thread kidney quarters and bacon-covered chestnuts alternately on to 4 skewers.

4. Stand in greased grill pan and brush with melted butter or margarine. Grill 3 minutes.

5. Turn over and brush with more butter or margarine. Grill a further 3 minutes. Serve hot with rice.

Shepherd's Pie with Chestnuts
Serves 8

The best Shepherd's Pie ever, the meat enhanced by the addition of chestnut purée and its topping, a froth of creamed potatoes flavoured with mustard. It goes well with lightly cooked shredded cabbage, Chinese leaves, sprouts and spring greens.

2 lb (900 g) lean minced beef
8 oz (225 g) onions, peeled and chopped
¾ pt (425 ml) water
2 to 3 level tsp salt
1 can (15½ oz or 439 g) Clèment Faugier chestnut purée
3 lb (1½ kg) freshly boiled potatoes
2 rounded tsp prepared mild mustard
2 oz (50 g) butter or margarine
¼ pt (150 ml) warm milk

1. Put beef into a pan, add onions then cook both together, uncovered, for ½ hour. Stir often to break up the meat and prevent it from forming a lump.

2. Pour in water then season with salt. Bring to boil, lower heat and cover. Simmer 1 hour, stirring from time to time.

3. Work in the chestnut purée. Reheat, stirring, until piping hot. Spoon into 5 pint (2.75 litre) dish.

4. Mash potatoes finely over low heat. Beat in mustard, butter or margarine and milk. Continue to beat until light and frothy. Pile over meat mixture. Reheat under hot grill until golden, or for 20 minutes in hot oven set to 425° F (220° C), Gas 7.

Beef and Hazelnut Stewpot
Serves 8 to 10

A worthwhile party piece and delicious with creamed

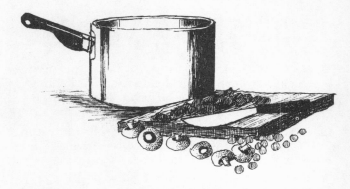

potatoes and a selection of mixed vegetables or a salad.

2 oz (50 g) butter or margarine
8 oz (225 g) onions, peeled and very thinly sliced
3½ to 4 lb (1¾ to 2 kg) cubed braising steak, washed and drained
4 oz (125 g) mushrooms, rinsed, drained, thinly sliced
1 can (11½ fluid oz or 330 ml) tomato and vegetable juice (V8) or plain tomato juice if preferred
2 to 3 level tsp salt
4 oz (125 g) hazelnuts
2 level tblsp plain flour
½ pt (275 ml) cold water

1. Sizzle butter or margarine in heavy-based saucepan. Add onions and fry over medium heat until warm gold.

2. Add meat cubes, a few at a time, and fry briskly until well-sealed and no longer red.

3. Mix in mushrooms, the juice, salt and hazelnuts. Bring to boil, stirring. Lower heat and cover pan. Simmer 1¾ to 2 hours or until meat is tender.

4. To thicken, mix flour smoothly with some of the water. Gradually blend in rest of water.

5. Add to beef mixture and cook gently, stirring, until mixture bubbles and thickens.

Brisket with Apricots and Walnuts
Serves 6 to 8

Fruity and fragrant, a delightful blend of flavours lend character to this beef braise which teams especially well with brown rice or boiled potatoes, and cauliflower coated with cheese sauce.

1 oz (25 g) butter or margarine
6 oz (175 g) onions, peeled and thinly sliced
2¼ to 2½ lb (1 to 1¼ kg) rolled brisket, as lean as possible and tied at ½ inch (1.25 cm) intervals
¾ pt (425 ml) boiling water
3 oz (75 g) broken walnut pieces
4 oz (125 g) dried apricots, soaked in boiling water for 2 hours
1½ level tsp salt
2 level tblsp flour
¼ pt (150 ml) cold water

1. Heat butter or margarine until sizzling in fairly large, heavy-based pan. Add onions and fry over a medium heat for 10 minutes or until golden brown.

2. Add whole piece of brisket and fry a little more briskly for 5 to 7 minutes, turning until all sides are well-sealed and brown.

3. Add boiling water, walnut pieces, drained apricots and salt. Bring to boil and skim. Lower heat and cover pan. Simmer 2½ to 3 hours or until meat is tender.

4. Transfer meat from pan to carving board. Remove string and slice. To thicken gravy, mix flour smoothly with some of the cold water. Stir in remainder.

5. Add to liquid in pan and bring to boil, stirring continuously. Replace sliced meat. Leave mixture overnight. Before serving, remove top layer of hard fat.

6. Bring gently to a slow boil and reheat for ¼ hour before serving.

Pork in African Mood
Serves 8

Thickened with bananas and mildly spiced, this is one of the finest pork dishes I know. Serve it with rice and a salad of red and green peppers mixed with chopped onions and enough sharpish French dressing to moisten.

3½ lb (1¾ kg) spare rib pork chops
2 oz (50 g) margarine or lard
4 oz (125 g) cashew nuts
10 oz (275 g) onions, peeled, chopped
4 oz (125 g) celery, scrubbed, chopped
12 oz (350 g) bananas
1 level tsp ground ginger
1 to 1½ level tsp cayenne pepper (fiery, so reduce for milder flavour)
2 to 3 level tsp salt
½ pt (275 ml) boiling water

1. Wash and dry chops. Remove bones and fat. Cut meat into 1 inch (2.5 cm) cubes.

2. Heat margarine or lard in heavy-based pan. Add nuts and fry until light gold. Stir in onions and celery. Cover.

3. Fry 8 minutes. Uncover and continue to fry a further 10 minutes or until ingredients turn golden brown.

4. Mix in pork cubes and fry briskly, stirring, for 6 minutes. Slice in bananas, stir well with pork and fry another 6 minutes.

5. Add all remaining ingredients. Bring to boil, stirring. Lower heat and cover. Simmer ¾ to 1 hour or until meat is cooked through and tender.

Note
Make as above, using 2½ lb (1 to 1.25 kg) diced chicken or turkey breast instead of pork. Simmer 30 to 40 minutes only.

Dressed Pork Loin Chops
Serves 4

The dressing in this instance is a homemade stuffing made from brown breadcrumbs, piled over meaty pork chops and baked in the oven. A winner with pasta and cauliflower.

4 pork loin chops, each weighing 8 oz or 225 g
1 oz (25 g) lard or margarine
1½ oz (40 g) onion, peeled and finely chopped
1½ oz (40 g) red or green pepper, finely chopped
water
4 oz (125 g) brown breadcrumbs
2 oz (50 g) walnuts, chopped
4 oz (125 g) trimmed mushrooms and stalks, washed, wiped dry, chopped
1 level tsp salt
1 Grade 2 egg, beaten
1 oz (25 g) extra butter or margarine, melted
watercress

1. Wash and dry chops, Heat lard or margarine in a large frying pan, add chops and fry over fairly brisk heat until golden brown and crisp on both sides.

2. Remove to a medium-sized roasting tin. For stuffing, boil the onion and pepper in water to cover for 5 minutes. Drain throughly.

3. In small basin, combine the onion and pepper with crumbs, walnuts, mushrooms, salt and beaten egg.

4. Mound over fleshy part of chops then trickle melted butter or margarine over the top of each. Cover with foil and cook ¾ hour in oven set to 400° F (200° C) Gas 6.

5. Uncover and continue to cook a further 15 to 20 minutes to brown and crispen the stuffing. Serve garnished with watercress.

Turkish-Style Pilav
Serves 4 to 6

The real thing, as I discovered on a gastronomic tour of Istanbul, is complex and best left in the capable hands of local chefs. My Pilav is an adaptation, as authentic as I could make it and, true to Eastern customs, elusively flavoured with cinnamon and pine nuts.

2 oz (50 g) butter or margarine
1 tblsp salad oil
1½ lb (675 g) lamb fillet, cut into small cubes
8 oz (225 g) onions, peeled, grated
8 oz (225 g) Italian round grain rice (now available as easy-cook)
1½ oz (40 g) pine nuts
2 level tblsp currants
1¼ pt (725 ml) chicken stock
1 level tsp salt
1 level tsp cinnamon
4 oz (125 g) blanched tomatoes, skinned, chopped

1. Sizzle butter or margarine and oil in a large pan. Add lamb, a few pieces at a time, and fry until well-sealed. Remove to plate with draining spoon.

2. Add onions and fry over medium heat until golden, allowing about 5 minutes. Stir in rice, nuts, currants and stock.

3. Replace lamb, season with salt and cinnamon then stir in tomatoes. Bring to boil, lower heat and cover.

4. Simmer over low heat for 30 to 35 minutes, the time depending very much on the rice. When ready, the grains should be plump and tender, all the liquid absorbed and the lamb cooked through.

5. Taste rice at this stage. If no liquid remains and grains are a little chewy, add ¼ pint (150 ml) extra boiling water and continue to simmer for an extra ¼ hour. Fork through then transfer to 4 warm plates and serve straight away.

Bobotie
Serves 4 to 6

A South African speciality composed of mildly curried lamb and a custardy topping sprinkled with almonds. It is made for freshly cooked rice and a popular vegetable combination; peas and carrots.

3 large slices white bread, de-crusted, cubed
8 tblsp milk
1½ oz (40 g) butter or margarine
8 oz (225 g) onions, peeled, grated
1 lb (450 g) lamb fillet or portion cut from leg, fat-trimmed, minced
4 slightly rounded tsp curry powder
1 level tsp caster sugar
1 tblsp vinegar
2 oz (50 g) seedless raisins
1½ oz (40 g) flaked almonds
1 level tsp salt
2 Grade 3 eggs

1. Tip bread into a bowl. Mix with 5 tablespoons milk and leave to soak for a good ½ hour. Beat until smooth, adding an extra tablespoon of milk if neccessary to give a thick, creamy mixture.

2. Heat butter or margarine in a pan. Add onions and fry until golden. Mix in raw lamb and fry fairly briskly for 7 to 10 minutes or until brown and crumbly.

3. Stir in curry powder, sugar, vinegar, raisins, 1 oz (25 g) flaked almonds and salt. Beat in the soaked bread and milk. Spread smoothly into a 2 pint (1 litre) greased heatproof dish.

4. Beat remaining milk with eggs. Pour over the lamb mixture then sprinkle with remaining nuts.

5. Bake, uncovered, for ¾ to 1¼ hours in cool oven, 325° F (160° C), Gas 3. When ready, the top should be a warm gold and the lamb mixture cooked through. Spoon out of dish to serve.

Stuffed Roast Lamb Leg
Serves 8 to 9

Grapefruit peel in a stuffing, with chopped bacon and brazil nuts, give it an original touch and 'lifts' the flavour of the lamb to perfection. This is very much a party dish, well-suited to Easter.

4 lb (2 kg) leg of lamb, boned out by an obliging butcher
4 oz (125 g) fresh white breadcrumbs
finely grated peel of 1 small washed and dried grapefruit
2 oz (50 g) onion, peeled, grated
2 oz (50 g) brazil nuts, chopped but not too finely
2 oz (50 g) streaky bacon, chopped, fried in its own fat until crisp
2 rounded tblsp chopped parsley
1 level tsp dried rosemary, crushed between finger and thumb
1 oz (25 g) butter or margarine, melted
1 level tsp salt
1 Grade 2 egg, beaten

1. Wash and dry lamb inside and out

2. Tip crumbs into a bowl. Mix in grapefruit peel, onions, brazil nuts, bacon, parsley, rosemary, butter or margarine and salt.

3. Fork in beaten egg to bind and add a few teaspoons of milk if necessary to hold stuffing together.

4. Pack into lamb, skewer opening together then stand joint in roasting tin. Roast 2 hours in moderate oven, 350° F (180° C), Gas 4, basting 3 or 4 times. Serve with gravy made from pan juices and a selection of seasonal vegetables.

Stuffed Roast Duck
Serves 4

Well wash a 4 lb (2 kg) oven-ready duck, thawed if frozen. Make stuffing as given above, substituting ½ level teaspoon dried sage for the rosemary and adding 2 oz (50 g) chopped preserved ginger in addition to the other ingredients. Sprinkle skin with salt and ground ginger. Roast exactly as above, allowing 1¾ to 2 hours. Do not baste.

SALADS

Grape and Pepper Salad

Serves 6

A novel salad, again refreshingly green and a winner with roast poultry.

½ medium head of curly endive, well-washed, dried
8 oz (225 g) grapes, peeled, halved, pips removed
3 oz (75 g) green pepper, washed, de-seeded, cut into strips, boiled for 3 minutes, drained
1 small onion, peeled, sliced, slices separated into rings
1 oz (25 g) flaked almonds, lightly roasted
French dressing

1. Tear endive into pieces and put into a salad bowl. Add grapes, pepper, onion rings and flaked almonds.

2. Toss with sufficient dressing to moisten.

Green as Grass Salad

Serves 4 to 6

An idea for midsummer, cooling to look at and refreshing to eat with meat, poultry and fish dishes.

8 oz (225 g) green peas, fresh or frozen, cooked, drained, left until cold
8 oz (225 g) sliced green runner beans, cooked, drained, left until cold
8 oz (225 g) green pepper, de-seeded, cut into strips, cooked 3 minutes in boiling water, drained
½ medium unpeeled cucumber, washed, dried, diced
leaves from 1 bunch of watercress, washed, drained, patted dry
2 large celery stalks, scrubbed, cut into thin diagonal slices
1 oz (25 g) butter or margarine
2 oz (50 g) brazil nuts, thinly sliced in food processor
French dressing

1. Put peas, beans, pepper, cucumber, watercress leaves and celery slices into a large mixing bowl.

2. Heat butter or margarine in a pan. Add brazils and fry until golden brown. Add to salad while hot and toss with sufficient French dressing to moisten. Transfer to a salad bowl.

Green Bean Croûton Salad

Serves 6

A simple salad contribution, well suited to egg, cheese and meat dishes.

1½ oz (40 g) butter or margarine
2 tsp salad oil
1 garlic clove, peeled, halved
2 slices de-crusted bread, cut into small cubes
1 lb (450 g) French beans, topped and tailed, cooked, drained, left to get cold
2 oz (50 g) onion, peeled, finely grated
2 oz (50 g) hazelnuts, finely chopped
French dressing

1. Heat butter or margarine with oil and garlic for 5 minutes in frying pan. Keep heat medium.

2. Remove garlic then add bread cubes to pan. Fry fairly briskly until golden brown and crisp. Lift out of pan and drain on kitchen paper.

3. Put beans into bowl. Add onion, hazelnuts and the fried bread cubes. Toss with sufficient dressing to moisten.

4. Transfer to a salad bowl and serve as suggested.

Aubergine and Pine Nut Salad
Serves 6

Try this one with kebabs tucked into warm pitta bread, with roast lamb, or with grilled and fried chicken.

1 lb (450 g) aubergines
boiling salted water
1 tblsp lemon juice
2 Grade 2 hardboiled eggs, shelled, coarsely grated
1 oz (25 g) pine nuts, lightly toasted
½ Webb or Cos lettuce, shredded, washed, dried
1 carton (5 oz or 142 ml) soured cream
2 tblsp natural yogurt
milk
1 level tsp salt
2 oz (50 g) black olives or 6 canned anchovies or 1 washed red pepper, de-seeded and cut into strips

1. Peel aubergines. Dice and cook in boiling salted water and lemon juice for 5 to 6 minutes or until only just tender. Keep pan covered throughout and avoid overcooking. Drain and cool completely.

2. Put into mixing bowl with two-thirds of the egg, pine nuts and lettuce.

3. Beat together soured cream and yogurt then thin down with milk to a thickish pouring consistency. Season with salt.

4. Add to salad and toss. Transfer to a serving bowl and garnish with either olives, anchovies or pepper strips and the remaining egg.

Waldorf Salad
Serves 6

A classic from America and a good companion to all kinds of poultry.

1 small Webb, Cos or Iceburg lettuce, shredded, washed, dried
2 tblsp French dressing
4 celery stalks, scrubbed, cut into thin diagonal slices
3 unpeeled red-skinned apples, washed, dried, quartered, cored, diced
3 oz (75 g) walnuts, coarsely chopped
¼ pt (150 ml) mayonnaise
5 tblsp natural yogurt
1 extra red-skinned apple
1 tblsp lemon juice

1. Divide lettuce equally between 6 individual salad bowls or dishes. Moisten with French dressing.

2. Transfer celery, diced apples and walnuts to mixing bowl. Toss with mayonnaise beaten with yogurt.

3. Spoon equal amounts into bowls over lettuce. Quarter last apple, remove core, leave unpeeled and cut into thin slices.

4. Brush with lemon juice to prevent browning then use to garnish salads.

Hawaiian Salad
Serves 6 to 8

Very much an 'all things bright and beautiful' salad, highly recommended for poultry and burgers.

1 can (about 13 oz or 375 g) crushed pineapple drained, juice kept for drinks
12 oz (350 g) carrots, peeled, grated
3 oz (75 g) seedless raisins
4 oz (125 g) white cabbage, very finely shredded
French dressing
1 oz (25 g) coarsely shredded coconut (thickish strips as opposed to desiccated), lightly toasted

1. Tip drained pineapple into a bowl. Add carrots, 2 oz (50 g) raisins, white cabbage and toss with sufficient French dressing to moisten.

2. Transfer to a salad bowl then sprinkle with coconut and remaining raisins.

Spanish Orange and Walnut Salad
Serves 4

Unbelievably simple, yet sophisticated enough to accompany duck, goose, pheasant and offal dishes.

6 large oranges
6 tblsp sweet sherry
1 oz (25 g) walnuts, chopped

1. Peel oranges and remove all traces of white pith. Cut into thin slices and remove pips.

2. Arrange fruit on 6 small plates. Coat with sherry, sprinkle with nuts and refrigerate for ½ hour before serving.

Sunshine Salad
Serves 6

A true brightener for almost any season of the year, with a refreshing tanginess that makes this a winner of a salad to serve with poultry, egg and cheese dishes. The surprise element here is a fruit and nut salad combined with French dressing.

1 medium pineapple, weighing about 2 lb (900 g to 1000 g)
3 oz (75 g) seedless raisins
2 oz (50 g) flaked almonds, toasted until golden brown

Dressing
2 tblsp bland salad oil
½ level tsp salt
½ level tsp caster sugar
1 level tsp prepared mild mustard
1½ tblsp vinegar

Garnish
watercress sprigs

1. Peel pineapple, removing 'eyes' with a potato peeler. Slice fruit then cut slices into small segments without removing centre core (which is usually the sweetest part of the fruit).

2. Transfer to mixing bowl. Add raisins and almonds. For dressing, beat oil with salt, sugar and mustard. Beat in vinegar and pour on to pineapple mixture.

3. Toss with two spoons and arrange in salad bowl. serve at room temperature, garnished with watercress.

Banana and Peanut Cream Salads
Serves 4

Nestling beneath a peanut butter dressing, these salads go extremely well with fish, poultry and offal dishes.

4 large bananas
lemon juice
4 lettuce-lined plates
2 level tblsp chunky peanut butter, at kitchen temperature
2 rounded tblsp soured cream
1½ tblsp fresh lime juice (about 1 lime)
½ level tsp celery salt
paprika

1. Peel bananas. Cut diagonally into thick slices. Sprinkle with lemon juice then put 1 sliced banana on to each plate.

2. For dressing, beat together peanut butter, soured cream and lime juice. Season with celery salt and extra salt as desired.

3. Spoon over bananas then garnish by sprinkling with paprika.

Grapefruit, Avocado and Cashew Salad
Serves 4 to 6

Fresh-tasting and fairly sharp, an appetising contrast to roast lamb and pork.

1 yellow grapefruit
1 pink grapefruit
1 large ripe avocado
1 oz (25 g) cashew nuts, lightly toasted, coarsely chopped
4 tblsp French dressing flavoured with ½ level tsp dried mint
1 heaped tblsp chopped parsley

1. Peel both grapefruit, removing all traces of white pith.

2. Holding each piece of fruit over a bowl to catch the juice, remove segments of flesh by cutting in between the membranes, the tough, dividing skin which holds the fruit together.

3. Peel avocado, halve and remove stone. Dice fruit. Add to bowl with toasted cashews. Toss ingredients together with French dressing and mint.

4. Divide salad equally between 4 or 6 dishes, sprinkle with parsley and serve lightly chilled.

Orange and Tomato Salad
Serves 4

Like a summer sunset, this is what I call an arranged salad, all the ingredients being placed on a large, flat plate then garnished and coated with dressing. It goes well with poultry and offal dishes. Also omelettes.

1 medium round lettuce, washed, leaves dried
1 head of chicory, washed, dried, separated into leaves
2 medium oranges, peeled, thinly sliced
4 medium tomatoes, blanched, skinned, sliced
12 radishes, topped and tailed, sliced
3 oz (75 g) onions, peeled, sliced, separated into rings
2 oz (50 g) brazil nuts, thinly sliced
4 to 5 tblsp French dressing

1. Cover a fairly large round plate with lettuce. Add a fringe of chicory leaves to resemble petals of a flower.

2. Fill centre with alternate slices of oranges and tomatoes.

3. Garnish with radishes, onion rings and brazil nuts then coat with dressing.

Courgette, Blue Cheese and Almond Salad
Serves 6

Uncoooked and unpeeled courgettes, tossed with blue cheese and nuts, make an original salad to serve with meat and fish dishes.

1 medium round lettuce, washed, drained, wiped dry
1 bunch spring onions, trimmed, washed, coarsely chopped
4 oz (125 g) firm blue cheese (such as Danish), cut into tiny dice or coarsely chopped
8 oz (225 g) unpeeled courgettes, topped and tailed, washed, dried, very thinly sliced
3 oz (75 g) blanched almonds, skinned, lightly toasted, chopped
1 garlic clove, peeled and crushed (optional)
4 to 5 tblsp French dressing flavoured with Worcester sauce

1. Tear lettuce into pieces and put into mixing bowl. Add onions, cheese, courgettes, 2 oz (50 g) almonds and garlic if used.
2. Add dressing. Toss thoroughly. Sprinkle with remaining nuts and serve as suggested.

Cracked Wheat and Cashew Salad
Serves 6 to 8

Make as Cracked Wheat and Cashews on page 68. When completely cold, stir in 3 tablespoons vinegar or lemon juice, 1 crushed garlic clove and 2 level teaspoons finely chopped fresh mint (the last ingredient is optional). Serve with eggs, poultry, meat, fish and cheese; also a stew of mixed vegetables.

Grand Hotel Potato Salad
Serves 8 to 10

Few can resist potato salad and this one is better than most with its assortment of surprise ingredients. Serve with meat, poultry, fish, egg and cheese dishes.

2 lb (900 g) potatoes, freshly cooked
3 oz (75 g) onion, peeled and very finely chopped
3 oz (75 g) green pepper, de-seeded and very finely chopped
4 rounded tblsp sweet pickle
4 celery stalks, scrubbed, thinly sliced
12 radishes, peeled, washed, very thinly sliced
6 Grade 3 hardboiled eggs, shelled and coarsely grated into bowl
¼ pt (150 ml) thick mayonnaise
1 level tsp prepared English mustard
5 oz (150g) natural yogurt
salt to taste
4 heaped tblsp chopped parsley

1. Dice potatoes and put into large bowl. Using a large spoon, toss in onion, green pepper, sweet pickle, celery, radishes and eggs.
2. Beat mayonnaise with mustard and yogurt. Add to potato mixture and stir gently with a spoon to mix. Season to taste.
3. Gently stir in half the parsley. Pile mixture in a serving dish and sprinkle rest of parsley over the top.

VEGETARIAN DISHES

Chestnut Cheese Casserole
Serves 4 to 6

I discovered this marvellous dish in a highly imaginative Twenties cook book and adapted it with great success. The author suggested serving it with cranberry sauce, a bright idea and a lovely contrast. Accompany with mange tout or baby peas and baked jacket potatoes.

8 oz (225 g) dried chestnuts, soaked overnight, drained
boiling water
1 tsp salt
1 oz (25 g) butter or margarine
8 oz (225 g) Cheddar cheese, grated
2 large slices brown bread, de-crusted, turned into crumbs

1. Put chestnuts into a pan. Add boiling water to cover then stir in salt.

2. Bring to boil, lower heat and cover. Simmer for ¾ to 1 hour or until chestnuts are tender. Drain. Rinse with cold water, drain again and break into small chunks.

3. Fill a 2 pint (1.25 litre) greased heatproof dish with alternate layers of chestnuts and cheese. End with cheese and sprinkle with breadcrumbs.

4. Bake 15 to 20 minutes in hot oven, 425° F (220° C), Gas 7. When ready, the mixture should be very hot and the top golden brown and crisp.

Cheesy Creamed Celeriac with Almonds
Serves 4

Unusual and filling, this is a delicately-flavoured main course using one of winter's best vegetables: celeriac with its gentle taste of celery and potato-like texture.

2 lb (900 g) celeriac
boiling salted water
juice of a small lemon
½ pt (275 ml) freshly made white sauce
3 oz (75g) Cheddar cheese, finely grated
2 level tsp curry powder
2 rounded tsp tubed or canned tomato purée
salt and pepper to taste
1 oz (25 g) fine white breadcrumbs
1 oz (25 g) ground almonds
2 oz (50 g) butter or margarine, melted

1. Peel celeriac thickly as flesh directly underneath skin is woody. Cut into cubes. Put into saucepan and cook in boiling salted water, with added lemon juice, for about ½ hour or until tender. Depending on the age, the celeriac may need longer. Drain, return to pan and keep hot.

2. Pour white sauce over celeriac then add 2 oz (50 g) cheese, curry powder, tomato purée and seasoning to taste. Mix thoroughly.

3. Transfer to a 2 pint (1.25 litre), greased heatproof dish. Sprinkle with rest of cheese mixed with crumbs and almonds. Trickle melted butter or margarine over the top.

4. Reheat and brown in hot oven, 450° F (230° C), Gas 8. Allow 20 to 25 minutes. Serve hot with salad.

Avocado Creamed Pasta with Pine Nuts

Serves 4 generously

A rich but easily made vegetarian-type main course, a joy with a topping of cheese and crunchy green salad to go with it.

1 packet (about 9 oz or 250 g) small pasta (such as baby shells recommended for soup)
boiling salted water
1 carton (5 oz or 142 ml) soured cream
2 oz (50 g) pine nuts, lightly toasted
1 medium-sized ripe avocado
salt and pepper to taste

1. Cook pasta in the boiling salted water as directed on the packet; it should take 10 to 12 minutes. Drain and return to saucepan. Stand over low heat.

2. Using a large spoon, mix in the soured cream and pine nuts, tossing mixture over and over.

3. Peel avocado as you would peel a pear, starting from the narrow end. Cut flesh into small cubes and gently fold into pasta mixture.

4. Adjust seasoning to taste and transfer to a warm serving dish. Hand grated Parmesan cheese separately for sprinkling over top of each portion.

Short-cut Pizza Neapolitan

Serves 2 to 3

Not quite the traditional Pizza made with a bread dough but a worthwhile variation based on the Cheese and Peanut Scone Round mixture page 58.

2 tblsp salad oil
4 oz (125 g) onions, peeled and chopped
2 level tblsp tomato purée
1 oz (25 g) salted peanuts, finely chopped
1 rounded tsp caster sugar
½ level tsp salt
1 rounded tsp dried basil
12 oz (350 g) blanched tomatoes
8 oz (225 g) Mozzarella cheese
Cheese and Peanut Scone Round mixture (page 58)
1½ oz (40 g) black olives

1. Heat oil in a pan. Add onions and fry until soft and pale gold. Mix in tomato purée, peanuts, sugar, salt and basil. Cool to lukewarm.

2. Thinly slice tomatoes and Mozzarella cheese. Roll out scone mixture into a 9 inch (22.5 cm) round. Transfer to a greased baking tray.

3. Spread with onion mixture then add a layer of sliced tomatoes. Finally top with Mozzarella cheese and stud with olives.

4. Bake until well-risen and bubbly in hot oven, 425° F (220° C), Gas 7. Allow about 25 to 30 minutes. Cut into wedges and serve hot.

Short-cut Mushroom Pizza

Serves 2 to 3

Make as previous recipe but garnish top with 2 oz (50 g) trimmed and sliced mushrooms tossed in 1 oz (25 g) melted butter or margarine. Instead of basil use thyme for flavouring.

Short-cut Pickled Onion Pizza

Make as Short-cut Pizza Neapolitan but sprinkle top with 6 oz (175 g) grated Cheddar cheese instead of Mozzarella. Garnish top with 6 large and thinly sliced pickled onions.

Mixed Fruit Platter
Serves 4

North American in concept, this kaleidescope of a cottage cheese and fruit assembly is also akin to the sort of lunchtime meal one might order at London's Fortnum and Mason. Elegant, pretty, fresh.

1 round lettuce, washed, dried
French dressing
12 oz (350 g) cottage cheese
3 oz (75 g) walnuts, coarsely chopped
4 oz (125 g) each, black and green grapes, washed, dried, separated into small clusters
8 oz (225 g) strawberries, washed and dried
8 oz (225 g) watermelon, cubed
1 small fresh pineapple, peeled, sliced, slices cut into small cubes
2 kiwi fruit, peeled and sliced
8 maraschino cherries

1. Use the large, outer leave of lettuce to cover a large plate. Shred remainder and sprinkle over the top. Moisten with French dressing.

2. Mix cheese and nuts together and mound on to centre of plate. Surround with the fruits. Decorate with maraschino cherries.

Cheese Puff Pudding
Serves 4

Soufflé-like and fairly economical to make, this is a worthwhile midweek dish served with baked tomato halves and mushrooms.

½ pt (275 ml) milk
4 oz (125 g) soft white breadcrumbs
4 oz (125 g) Cheddar cheese, finely grated
1 level tsp prepared mustard
1 level tsp mild curry powder
2 oz (50 g) onion, peeled and finely grated
1 level tsp salt
1 level tsp paprika
1½ oz (40 g) salted peanuts, coarsely chopped
2 Grade 2 eggs, separated
¼ tsp vinegar

1. Well-grease a 2½ pint (1.5 litre) deep heatproof dish. Set oven to moderately hot, 375°F (190° C), Gas 5.

2. Heat milk in fairly large saucepan until lukewarm. Mix in crumbs and stir over medium heat until thick and smooth.

3. Gently beat in cheese, mustard, curry powder, onion, salt, paprika, peanuts and egg yolks.

4. Whisk egg whites and vinegar to a stiff snow. Using a large metal spoon or spatula, fold gently into breadcrumb mixture until smooth and evenly combined.

5. Pour into prepared dish and bake 35 to 40 minutes or until well-risen and golden brown. Serve straight away.

Hazelnut and Blue Cheese Quiche
Serves 6

Related to more traditional Quiches, this one has a crisp and short hazelnut pastry and a filling containing Britain's most renowned cheese — Stilton. It is somewhat rich and extravagent so reserve for special occasions.

6 oz (175 g) plain flour
pinch of salt
3½ oz (90 g) mixture of white vegetable cooking fat with
butter or margarine
1 oz (25 g) hazelnuts, very finely ground
3 tblsp cold water to mix
3 oz (75 g) firm Stilton cheese, cut into tiny cubes
½ pt (275 ml) single cream
3 Grade 3 eggs
salt and pepper to taste

1. For pastry, sift flour and salt into bowl. Rub in fats
   finely then toss in hazelnuts.

2. Using a fork, mix to a stiff pastry with the cold water.
   Roll out fairly thinly on a floured surface then use to
   line an 8 inch (20 cm) fluted pottery flan dish, first
   lightly greased.

3. Sprinkle cheese over the base. Beat cream and eggs
   well together then season to taste with salt and
   pepper.

4. Pour into flan dish over cheese then bake 10 minutes
   in hot oven, 425° F (220° C), Gas 7.

5. Reduce temperature to moderate, 350° F (180° C),
   Gas 4, and continue to bake a further 25 to 30 minutes
   or until filling is set and pastry pale gold. Cut into
   wedges and serve warm or cold with salad.

Note
*Stand flan dish on a metal baking tray in the oven as it will
help the pastry to crispen more evenly over the base.*

Cheese 'Schnitzels'
Allow 2 per person (Serves 4)

Although I have used a similar recipe to this before, I
admit I have no inkling where the idea came from. Only
that it's very good indeed and worth repeating. Serve
with fried potatoes and a selection of cooked vegetables
or a mixed salad.

8 slices of packeted processed cheese
plain flour
3 Grade 3 eggs
½ level tsp salt
½ level tsp celery salt
1 level tsp powder mustard
½ tsp Worcester sauce
3 oz (75 g) lightly toasted white breadcrumbs
1 oz (25 g) ground almonds
(mix breadcrumbs and ground almonds together on piece of
greaseproof paper)
about 4 inches (10 cm) oil for frying (use a deepish frying
pan)
lemon wedges and parsley for garnishing

1. Separate cheese slices and coat first in flour then in
   eggs, beaten thoroughly with salt, celery salt, mustard
   and Worcester sauce.

2. Ensure both sides of each cheese slice are well-
   covered then dip into the crumb and almond mixture.
   Leave to stand ¼ hour. Re-coat with egg and crumb
   mixture. Stand ½ hour in the refrigerator to give
   coating a chance to 'set'.

3. Do not pile cheese slices on top of the other but spread
   out on to a large plate. Heat oil until a cube of bread
   sinks to the bottom of the pan, browns in ½ a minute
   and rises to the top. Remove and discard.

4. Add cheese 'Schnitzels', 2 at a time, and fry for ¾
   minute only. Remove from pan, drain on crumpled
   kitchen paper and serve hot, garnished with lemon
   and parsley.

Cheese and Peanut Scone Round
Makes 8

Whether served simply enough with a filling of butter or peanut butter, or eaten with egg dishes, these scone triangles are a sheer joy freshly baked. Quite delicious and a nourishing meal with a robust mixed salad.

8 oz (225 g) self-raising flour
1 level tsp baking powder
1 level tsp salt
1 level tsp powder mustard
1 oz (25 g) butter, margarine or white vegetable cooking fat
3 oz (75 g) Cheddar cheese, finely grated
1½ oz (40 g) salted peanuts, finely chopped
¼ pt (150 ml) cold milk
beaten egg for brushing

1. Sift flour, baking powder, salt and mustard into a mixing bowl. Rub in fat finely.

2. Toss in cheese and nuts. Add milk *in one go* and mix to a soft dough by stirring with a fork.

3. Turn out on to a floured surface, knead quickly and lightly until smooth then shape into a ball. Place on greased baking tray.

4. Using floured fingers or rolling pin, press out to ¾ inch (2 cm) in thickness. Score into 8 wedges with the back of a knife.

5. Brush with beaten egg and bake until golden brown in hot oven, 425° F (220° C), Gas 7. Allow about 15 to 20 minutes.

6. Transfer to wire rack and leave until lukewarm. Divide into triangles, using score lines as a guide.

7. Serve when just cold by breaking each triangle in half and spreading with butter, margarine or peanut butter.

Poppy or Sesame Seed Scone Round
Makes 8

Make as above. After brushing with egg, sprinkle with 4 to 5 level teaspoons poppy or sesame seeds.

Spanish Rice
Serves 4 to 6

Mounded with grated cheese and accompanied by a mixed salad or cooked greens, this is a thoroughly enjoyable dish containing almonds, southern Europe's favourite nut.

8 oz (225 g) easy-cook, long grain rice
½ pt (275 ml) tomato juice
½ pt (275 ml) boiling water
3 oz (75 g) each, red and green pepper, de-seeded and chopped
3 oz (75 g) onion, peeled and grated
2 level tsp salt
2 oz (50 g) blanched almonds, skinned, lightly toasted, chopped

1. Put rice into a saucepan with tomato juice, boiling water, red and green pepper, onion, salt and two-thirds of the nuts.

2. Bring to boil, lower heat and cover. Simmer 15 to 20 minutes or until grains are plump and tender and have absorbed all the liquid.

3. Fluff up with a fork, tip into a serving dish and sprinkle rest of nuts on top.

Stuffed Aubergines Louisiana
Serves 4

Adapted from some of the vivacious dishes I discovered in this unique part of the USA, this is a fine, full-flavoured aubergine dish which goes well with fried tomatoes.

2 large aubergines (2 lb or 900 g)
2 oz (50 g) butter or margarine
1 tblsp salad oil
4 oz (125 g) onion, peeled and grated
2 large celery stalks, scrubbed, chopped
3 oz (75 g) green pepper, washed, de-seeded, chopped
3 oz (75 g) trimmed mushrooms, washed, rinsed, chopped
1 garlic clove, peeled and crushed
2 oz (50 g) fresh brown breadcrumbs
1 rounded tblsp tomato purée
2 oz (50 g) pecan nuts, chopped
4 oz (125 g) Cheddar cheese, grated
½ oz (15 g) extra butter or margarine, melted

1. Wash and dry aubergines and halve lengthwise. Scoop out flesh, leaving ¼ inch (5 mm) thick 'shells'. Chop flesh fairly finely. Cook 'shells' in boiling salted water for 5 minutes. Drain.

2. Heat butter or margarine and oil until sizzling. Add chopped aubergine flesh, onions, celery, pepper, mushrooms and garlic.

3. Fry, uncovered, over a medium heat for about 15 to 20 minutes or until aubergine is tender and mixture golden brown.

4. Stir in crumbs to thicken then add tomato purée, two-thirds of the nuts and half the cheese.

5. Pile smoothly into aubergine 'shells', sprinkle with remaining cheese and nuts and trickle extra butter or margarine on top of each. Stand in a well-greased baking tin then re-heat and brown 20 minutes in moderately hot oven, 400° F (200° C), Gas 6.

Mixed Nut Loaf

Hot with gravy and vegetables or cold with salad, the loaf is appealing anyway it's served and leftovers make a tempting, munchy sandwich filling with lettuce and cucumber.

4 oz (125 g) peanuts, lightly toasted, skins rubbed off
2 oz (50 g) walnuts
1 oz (25 g) pine nuts
1 oz (25 g) cashews
6 oz (175 g) brown breadcrumbs
3 oz (75 g) onion, peeled and grated
1 level tsp finely grated lemon peel
4 heaped tblsp chopped parsley
2 level tsp salt
3 tblsp hot milk
1 Grade 3 egg, beaten
1 tsp Worcester sauce

1. Finely grind nuts in food processor or blender goblet. Tip into a bowl and toss in crumbs, onion, lemon peel, parsley and salt.

2. Bind together with milk, egg and Worcester sauce, stirring with a fork.

3. With damp hands, shape into a 2 inch (5 cm) high loaf. Stand on baking tray lined with greased foil. Bake ¾ hour in moderate oven set to 350° F (180° C), Gas 4.

Tip
If mixture is on the dry side, add a little more milk. If too wet, stir in extra crumbs.

Nutty Burgers

One of the delights of vegetarian cuisine, these Nutty Burgers are exceptionally good, even if not 100% original. Serve them between warm burger buns, smothered with mild mustard or relish. Or eat them cold with salad.

2 oz (50 g) brazil nuts
2 oz (50 g) ground almonds
½ level tsp powder mustard
3 oz (75 g) brown breadcrumbs
3 oz (75 g) onion, peeled and finely grated
1 level tsp yeast extract such as Marmite or Vecon
1 level tsp mixed herbs
1 Grade 2 egg, beaten
2 tblsp hot milk
seasoning to taste
margarine, vegetable fat or corn oil for frying

1. Finely grind brazil nuts in food processor or blender. Tip into mixing bowl. Add almonds, mustard, crumbs, onion, yeast extract and herbs.

2. Bind together with egg and milk, stirring with a fork. Season to taste with salt and pepper. Shape into 8 burgers with damp hands. Leave to stand ½ hour to firm-up.

3. Heat about ¼ inch (5 mm) melted fat or oil in frying pan. Add burgers and fry until golden brown, allowing about 5 to 6 minutes and turning twice.

4. Remove from pan, drain on crumpled paper towels and eat hot or cold.

Cheesy Wagon Wheels
Makes about 14

Made from my own version of mock puff pastry, these have been especially designed for children with two of their top favourites — peanuts and tomato ketchup! The Wagon Wheels are non-junky and well-endowed with protein; an attractive addition to the lunch, high tea or supper table.

8 oz (225 g) self-raising flour
½ level tsp salt
6 oz (175 g) mixture of margarine and white vegetable cooking fat
7 tblsp cold milk
2 rounded tblsp tomato ketchup
4 oz (125 g) Cheddar cheese, grated
2 oz (50 g) salted peanuts, finely chopped
1 Grade 4 egg for brushing, well-beaten

1. Sift flour and salt into a bowl. Cut in fats until they look like baby peas. Add milk in *one go* and draw mixture together with fingertips.

2. Turn out on to a lightly floured surface and knead briefly until smooth. Wrap and refrigerate ½ hour.

3. Roll out fairly thinly into a rectangle measuring 15 by 10 inches (37.5 cm by 25 cm). Spread with tomato ketchup, taking it to edges of pastry.

4. Sprinkle cheese over the top, followed by the nuts. Roll up, starting from one of the longer sides. Cut into 14 slices.

5. Transfer to 2 well-greased baking trays and brush with egg. Bake 1 shelf above and 1 shelf below oven centre set to hot, 425° F (220° C), Gas 7.

6. Allow about 12 to 15 minutes and reverse position of trays half way through baking. Cool on a wire rack. Eat when warm for preference.

5. Pile equal amounts neatly into courgette halves then trickle rest of melted butter or margarine over tops of each.

6. Reheat and brown for 10 to 15 minutes in hot oven, 425° F (220° C), Gas 7.

Stuffed Courgettes
Serves 4

A light main course for summer, pleasant with grilled tomato halves.

8 courgettes (1½ lb or 675 g)
boiling water
salt
4 oz (125 g) dried apricots, soaked overnight
6 oz (175 g) soft brown breadcrumbs
3 oz (75 g) onion, peeled and grated
2 oz (50 g) walnuts, coursely chopped
1 rounded tblsp finely chopped parsley
1 level tsp celery salt
1 Grade 2 egg
3 tblsp milk
2 oz (50 g) butter or margarine, melted
seasoning to taste

1. Top and tail courgettes. Wash and halve lengthwise. Carefully scoop out centre seeds, taking care not to break through courgette shells.

2. Place shells in large frying pan or saucepan, add boiling water to cover and sprinkle with salt. Bring to boil, lower heat and cook 6 minutes. Drain. Arrange on greased baking tray.

3. To make stuffing, drain apricots and snip into tiny pieces with scissors. Transfer to mixing bowl. Add crumbs, onion, walnuts, parsley and celery salt.

4. Bind together with egg, milk and half the butter or margarine. Mix thoroughly. Season to taste.

Curried Lentils
Serves 6 to 8

Accompanied with rice and side dishes of chutney, yogurt and chopped-up tomatoes and cucumber, this is bound to please all nut-loving vegetarians who are curry addicts at the same time!

8 oz (225 g) bright orange lentils
2 oz (50 g) butter or margarine
2 tsp salad oil
2 garlic cloves, peeled and crushed
8 oz (225 g) onions, peeled and grated
4 oz (125 g) unsalted peanuts, toasted, skins rubbed off,
nuts coarsely chopped
2 level tblsp curry powder
1 level tsp turmeric
1 level tsp paprika
2 level tsp fresh ginger, peeled and finely chopped or
squeezed through a garlic press
seeds from 3 opened-out cardamom pods
2 level tblsp tomato purée
1¼ pt (725 ml) boiling water
2 level tsp salt
2 level tblsp chopped fresh coriander leaves or parsley

1. Rinse lentils and leave on one side for the time being.

2. Heat butter or margarine and oil in large pan. Add garlic and onions. Fry until a warm gold, stirring from time to time. Add lentils.

3. Mix in peanuts, curry powder, turmeric, paprika, ginger, cardamom seeds, tomato purée, boiling water and salt.

4. Bring to boil and lower heat. Cover pan and simmer about 45 minutes to 1 hour or until lentil mixture is thick and has absorbed most of the liquid.

5. Stir frequently and top up with extra boiling water if lentils seem to be thickening up too much. Turn into a serving dish and sprinkle with the fresh coriander or parsley.

ACCOMPANIMENTS

Harlequin Pineapple Slices
Serves 4

Try these with an American-style meal of burgers and jacket potatoes topped with butter or margarine. They are splendidly rich yet piquant at the same time, a most unusual accompaniment.

4 by 1 inch (2.5 cm) thick slices of fresh peeled pineapple
(do not remove centre core)
2 tblsp green peppermint liqueur
4 heaped tblsp soured cream
2 oz (50 g) pecan nuts, finely ground
4 fresh strawberries, washed, stalks left in

1. Place pineapple slices on 4 individual plates and coat with liqueur.

2. Top with soured cream and shower with the pecans. Garnish each with a strawberry.

Brussels Sprouts and Chestnuts
Serves 8

A much-loved accompaniment, particularly with poultry.

1 lb (450 g) chestnuts
1 lb (450 g) Brussels sprouts
2 oz (50 g) butter or margarine

1. Make a deep cut in the flat side of each chestnut and cook ¾ to 1 hour in boiling salted water. Drain chestnuts then take off peel and brown skin. Break each one into 4 or 5 pieces.

2. About ½ hour before serving, trim sprouts and make a cross cut in the base of each. Soak for 10 minutes in cold water. Drain. Cook for 10 to 12 minutes only in boiling salted water. Drain.

3. Melt butter or margarine in a large pan. Add chestnuts and sprouts. Leave over medium heat and toss over and over until piping hot. Serve straight away.

Corn and Peanut Fritters

Makes 12 to 16

Designed for poultry, these fritters are superb served hot and are especially recommended as an accompaniment to Chicken Maryland and ready-prepared packets of Chicken Kiev or Chicken Cordon Bleu.

4 oz (125 g) self-raising flour
½ level tsp salt
½ level tsp powder mustard
pinch of cayenne pepper
1 Grade 3 egg
¼ oz (10 g) melted butter or margarine
¼ pt (150 ml) cold milk
4 rounded tblsp cooked and drained sweetcorn
1 oz (25 g) salted peanuts, chopped
shallow fat or oil for frying

1. Sift flour, salt, mustard and pepper into a bowl.

2. Beat in whole egg and butter or margarine. Whisk in milk to make a smooth, thick batter.

3. Stir in sweetcorn and peanuts. Brush a heavy-based frying pan (non-stick for preference) with melted fat or oil.

4. Heat until very hot then pour off surplus into a cup or fritters will stick.

5. Drop small mounds of mixture, about 4 at a time, into pan. Flatten slightly then cook until bubbles break on the surface and undersides are golden brown. Flip over and cook second sides until golden.

6. Repeat, using up all the mixture. Place Fritters, as they are cooked, between folds of a tea towel to keep warm. Serve as suggested.

Italian Walnut and Parmesan Gnocchi

Serves 4 to 6

A classy accompaniment for lamb and poultry dishes. It has, as its base, semolina and may also be served as a main course with creamed spinach and grilled tomato halves.

1 pt (575 ml) milk
5 oz (150 g) semolina
1 level tsp salt
2 oz (50 g) butter or margarine
3 oz (75 g) Cheddar cheese, grated
2 oz (50 g) finely grated Parmesan cheese
2 oz (50 g) walnuts, finely chopped
1 Grade 1 or 2 egg, beaten

1. Pour milk into a heavy-based saucepan. Add semolina, salt and half the butter or margarine.

2. Slowly bring to the boil, stirring continuously. Continue to cook moderately for a further 3 minutes when mixture will be very thick.

3. Remove from heat and beat in 2 oz (50 g) Cheddar cheese and 1 oz (25 g) Parmesan cheese, the walnuts and egg. Return to heat and cook slowly, stirring all the time, for a further 2 minutes.

4. Spread into a greased Swiss roll tin and smooth top with a knife dipped in water. Cover loosely with foil and refrigerate until firm.

5. Cut into 1 inch (2.5 cm) squares and arrange, in layers, in a greased, 2 pint (1 litre) shallow, heatproof dish.

6. Dot with flakes of remaining butter or margarine, sprinkle with rest of the cheeses and reheat and brown for 15 to 20 minutes in a moderately hot oven, 400° F (200° C), Gas 6. Spoon out of dish to serve.

Pasta Nut Cream
Serves 6

I first served this somewhat unusual pasta dish with roast beef and then tried it with roast lamb and chicken. It went beautifully with all and made a welcome change from potatoes. It is now an established favourite.

8 oz (225 g) broken macaroni, pasta shells or pasta bows
boiling salted water
2 tsp salad oil
2 oz (50 g) hazelnuts, chopped
2 oz (50 g) Cheddar cheese, grated
¼ pt (150 ml) single cream
1 Grade 2 egg
salt and pepper to taste

1. Cook macaroni, shells or bows in salted water and oil as directed on the packet. Drain. Return to pan and stand over low heat.

2. Add hazelnuts and cheese. Beat cream and egg well together. Mix gently into pasta and cook for 2 minutes or until egg sets very lightly, tossing gently over and over with a large spoon.

3. Season well to taste with salt and freshly milled pepper and serve straight away.

Orange Cranberry Nut Relish
Serves 12 to 16

From across the Atlantic comes this typical winter relish, always served with the Thanksgiving turkey in November. I've adapted the recipe from one given to me by the Chef at the Vista International hotel in downtown New York.

2 small unpeeled oranges, washed and dried
1 lb (450 g) fresh or frozen cranberries
4 oz (125 g) pecan nuts
12 oz (350 g) caster sugar

1. Quarter oranges and remove pips. Mince fairly finely with cranberries and nuts. Alternatively, use a blender or food processor.

2. Transfer to a bowl and stir in sugar. Spoon into jars, cover with cling film and refrigerate until needed. The relish may also be deep frozen.

Orange Peanut Rice
Serves 4 to 6

Unusually fragrant with poultry, lamb, offal and veal.

1 oz (25 g) butter or margarine
2 oz (50 g) onion, peeled and grated
8 oz (225 g) easy-cook, long grain rice
1 pt (575 ml) chicken, beef or vegetable stock
1½ level tsp orange peel
2 oz (50 g) salted peanuts, chopped
salt and pepper to taste
1 oz (25 g) extra butter or margarine (optional)

1. Heat butter or margarine in fairly large saucepan. Add onion and fry gently until pale but still soft. Allow about 7 minutes and keep pan covered throughout.

2. Add rice and cook 2 more minutes, stirring. Pour in stock then add orange peel and nuts.

3. Bring to boil, lower heat and cover. Cook undisturbed for 15 to 20 minutes or until grains are plump and tender and have absorbed all the liquid.

4. Fork in seasoning to taste and the butter or margarine. Serve hot.

Apple, Lemon and Walnut Sauce

Part of the smart set, this one, and outstandingly good with pork and bacon dishes.

1 lb (450 g) cooking apples, peeled, quartered, cored, thinly sliced
4 tblsp cold water
2 level tblsp caster sugar
1 level tsp finely grated lemon peel
1 oz (25 g) walnuts, finely chopped

1. Put apples into saucepan with water. Cook to a pulp over a low heat. Keep covered and watch carefully to ensure apples do not burn.

2. Beat to a purée with a spoon, or do so in blender goblet or food processor. Return to pan. Add sugar and lemon peel.

3. Heat gently, stirring, until sugar dissolves. Mix in walnuts. Transfer to a bowl. Serve when completely cold.

Brown Bread Sauce with Pecans
Serves 6 to 8

Pecans and cream make this re-vamped sauce on the costly side but it is a gastronomic treat with turkey, chicken and pheasant and a welcome change from traditional bread sauce.

½ pt (275 ml) cold milk
1 large onion, peeled, halved
2 bouquet garni sachets
1 level tsp salt
3 oz (75 g) fresh brown breadcrumbs
1 oz (25 g) pecan nuts, very finely chopped
1 oz (25 g) butter or margarine
3 tblsp double cream
white pepper to taste

1. Pour milk into saucepan. Add onion, bouquet garni sachets and salt. Bring just up to the boil, cover and leave to stand 1 hour so that flavours mingle.

2. Strain milk, through a fine mesh sieve, into a clean pan. Add crumbs, pecan nuts, butter or margarine, cream and pepper to taste.

3. Stir over a low heat until thick and very hot. Serve straight away.

Three Nut Mayonnaise
Makes just over ½ pint (275 ml)

For those who are devotees of both nuts and mayonnaise, this one is sure to please with its mixture of ground nuts, fresh parsley and garlic. Try it as a dressing for fried fish, grilled salmon, scampi and poached sea bass. Or just spoon it over crisp lettuce hearts for a very easy but sophisticated salad. Or serve as an accompaniment to freshly cooked French beans.

½ pt (275 ml) thick mayonnaise
1 oz (25 g) each, *hazelnuts, walnuts and brazil nuts,* all
finely ground in blender or food processor
1 rounded tblsp finely chopped parsley
1 garlic clove, peeled and crushed
seasoning to taste

1. Mix all ingredients well together

2. Transfer to a small dish and use as suggested.

Cracked Wheat and Cashews
Serves 6 to 8

Characterfully Middle Eastern, this accompaniment has
a dual personality. Served hot, it teams well with egg and
poultry dishes; served cold, with just three extras, it
converts into a tasty and full-textured salad with a
pleasing 'bite' (see page 52). Cracked wheat is also known
as bulgar, bulgur and burghul, and available from health
food shops and some supermarket chains.

1 tblsp salad oil
8 oz (225 g) cracked wheat
4 oz (125 g) lightly toasted cashews
1 pt (575 ml) cold water
3 level tsp salt
2 heaped tblsp chopped parsley

1. Heat salad oil until hot and sizzling in saucepan. Add
cracked wheat and fry over medium heat for 5
minutes or until golden, turning frequently.

2. Stir in cashews, water and salt. Bring to boil, lower
heat and cover tightly. Simmer about ¼ hour or until
wheat has absorbed all the liquid. Stir occasionally.
Fork in parsley and serve while still very hot.

Brandy Butter
Serves 6 to 8

Old-fashioned perhaps, but certainly traditional with the
addition of ground almonds.

4 oz (125 g) unsalted butter, at kitchen temperature
2 oz (50 g) light brown soft sugar
2 oz (50 g) caster sugar
6 tsp brandy
1 oz (25 g) ground almonds
mixed spice

1. Beat butter with both sugars until light in texture,
very creamy and much paler in colour.

2. Stir in brandy and almonds. Pipe or spoon into a small
serving dish and sprinkle with spice. Refrigerate until
firm before serving.

Rum Butter
Serves 6 to 8

Make exactly as above, substituting rum for brandy, and
sprinkling top with ground ginger or nutmeg.

Desserts

Creamy Cheese Crunch Cake

What bliss! The creamiest of creamy cheese cakes baked atop a buttery, biscuity nut base. For fruit cheesecake, top with any fruit pie filling to taste.

3 oz (75 g) milk chocolate digestive biscuits, crushed
1 oz (25 g) blanched and toasted almonds or brazil nuts,
finely chopped
2 oz (50 g) butter, melted
2 oz (50 g) light brown soft sugar

Filling
1½ lb (675 g) curd cheese or tubs of low fat cream cheese
from France or Germany
6 oz (175 g) caster sugar
finely grated peel and juice of 1 small washed and dried
lemon
2 level tblsp cornflour
1 tsp vanilla essence
4 oz (125 g) butter, melted
2 level tblsp cornflour

1. Well-grease an 8 inch (20 cm) spring-clip tin with melted butter or margarine.

2. Mix together biscuits, nuts, butter and sugar and sprinkle thickly over base of tin.

3. Beat cheese until creamy then work in all remaining ingredients. Whip until very smooth.

4. Pour into tin over crumbs, spread top evenly with a knife and bake 1¼ to 1½ hours in a cool oven, 300° F (150° C), Gas 3.

5. Cake is ready when filling is firm and set — rather like a baked egg custard.

6. Remove from oven and leave until completely cold before unclipping sides of tin. Leave on tin base for serving.

Butto-Choc Banana Sundaes
Serves 4

Sumptuous and rich, the butterscotch sauce contributes a new flavour to these Banana Sundaes — as does the chocolate ice cream.

4 large bananas
a little lemon juice
2 oz (50 g) butter
1½ oz (40 g) light brown soft sugar
2 oz (50 g) marshmallows
1 tblsp milk
about ¾ pt (½ litre) chocolate ice cream
¼ pt (150 ml) double cream, whipped
1 oz (25 g) walnuts, chopped

1. Peel bananas and slice directly into 4 sundae dishes. Sprinkle with a little lemon juice to prevent browning.

2. For sauce, put butter, sugar, marshmallows and milk into a saucepan. Stir over a low heat until ingredients melt.

3. Bring to the boil and boil steadily for about 3 to 4 minutes or until sauce starts to thicken.

4. Top bananas with scoops or slices of ice cream, pile high with cream, coat with sauce and sprinkle with nuts. Serve straight away.

Peachy Nut Sundaes
Serves 4

Make the Sauce as above. Stand 4 large canned peach halves into 4 sundae glasses. Pile high with vanilla ice cream. Coat with the Butterscotch Sauce then sprinkle with 1 oz (25 g) flaked and lightly toasted almonds, coarsely crushed.

Real Trifle
Serves 8 to 10

Rather like real ale, this is a gem from the past, delighting everyone of all ages since Victorian times.

1 pt (575 ml) milk
4 Grade 3 eggs
2 Grade 3 egg yolks
2 oz (50 g) caster sugar
1 tsp vanilla essence
1 level tblsp cornflour
6 oz (175 g) sponge cake, cut into cubes
8 tblsp sweet sherry
4 rounded tblsp raspberry jam
2 oz (50 g) flaked almonds, lightly toasted
½ pt (275 ml) double cream
2 extra level tblsp caster sugar
2 oz (50 g) glacé cherries, sliced

1. Beat first 6 ingredients well together. Pour into a heavy-based pan. Cook, whisking gently all the time, until sauce, just, but only just, comes up to the boil and thickens. At once pour into a bowl and whisk until lukewarm. To prevent custard overcooking, heat until thick in a double pan or in basin over a pan of boiling water, whisking occasionally. The choice of method depends on your confidence!

2. Mix lukewarm custard with cake, sherry, jam and half the almonds. Press smoothly into a glass serving dish. Cover. Refrigerate until well-chilled.

3. Before serving, whisk cream until thick. Stir in sugar, swirl over top of trifle and finally sprinkle with remaining almonds. Stud with sliced cherries and serve by spooning out of dish.

Desert Sands Fruit Salad
Serves 6

An exotic winter fruit salad, fragrant with rose essence and apricot brandy.

2 large oranges, peeled, all white pith removed, sliced
6 oz (175 g) grapes, halved, pips removed
6 oz (175 g) fresh dates, skins and stones removed, halved
2 large bananas
1½ oz (40 g) pine nuts
4 tblsp apricot brandy
½ tsp rose essence
1 tblsp lemon juice

1. Cut oranges into small wedges. Put into bowl. Add grapes and halved dates.

2. Peel bananas and slice directly into bowl. Stir in remaining ingredients.

3. Cover. Refrigerate 3 to 4 hours. Bring back to room temperature before serving with sponge cakes or fingers.

Coconut Orange Paradise
Serves 4

Simple in the classic sense, a light and bright sweet to serve after a heavy meal. The whisky adds the finishing touch.

6 large oranges
3 level tblsp golden syrup
3 tblsp whisky
2 rounded tblsp desiccated coconut

1. Peel oranges and remove all traces of white pith. Cut into slices, catching juice in a bowl.

2. Put juice, syrup and whisky into a pan. Stir over a low heat until syrup melts, but do not allow to boil.

3. Layer orange slices in a heatproof dish (glass for preference), coating each layer with the melted syrup mixture.

4. Finally sprinkle with coconut and brown under a hot grill. Cool then refrigerate at least 2 hours before serving.

Nut Snow Cream

½ pt (275 ml) double cream
2 level tblsp caster sugar
1 tblsp whisky, brandy or orange-flavoured liqueur
1½ oz (40 g) very finely chopped walnuts, blanched and toasted almonds or blanched pistachios
1 egg white
2 or 3 drops of lemon juice

1. Whip cream until thick. Stir in sugar, spirit or liqueur and nuts.

2. Beat egg white and lemon juice to a stiff snow. Fold into cream and serve.

Advocaat Strawberry Creams
Serves 4

A dream of a sweet in which advocaat and walnuts play a major rôle. For 8 servings, double all the ingredients and you will have a sweet fit for any dinner party.

8 oz (225 g) strawberries, washed, hulled, sliced
4 level tblsp caster sugar
4 tblsp fresh orange juice
¼ pt (150 ml) double cream
2 oz (50 g) walnuts, chopped
5 tblsp advocaat

1. Toss strawberries with sugar and orange juice. Divide equally between 4 wine-type glasses.

2. Whip double cream until thick. Fold in 1½oz (40 g) walnuts and the advocaat. Pile over strawberries in dish then sprinkle with remaining walnuts.

3. Chill lightly in the refrigerator before serving with fan-shaped wafers.

Danish Apple 'Cake'
Serves 4

Also known, sometimes, as Peasant Girl with Veil, this so-called cake is anything but, and is a layered dessert made from apples and crumbs. I have adapted this recipe from an original Danish one.

1½ lb (675 g) cooking apples, peeled, quartered, cored, thinly sliced
4 tblsp water
3 oz (75 g) caster sugar
2 oz (50 g) butter or margarine
4 oz (125 g) fresh brown breadcrumbs
2 oz (50 g) blanched almonds, skinned, lightly toasted, finely chopped
2 oz (50 g) light brown soft sugar
¼ pt (150 ml) double cream
1 tblsp cold milk
4 tsp plum jam

1. Cook apples and water in covered saucepan until soft and pulpy, watching carefully in case they stick. For this reason, keep heat moderate and stir once. If Bramley apples are used, they will puff up in the saucepan when ready.

2. Beat to a purée with a fork, whisk or wooden spoon. Alternatively, work to a purée in blender or food processor. Stir in sugar and return to a saucepan. Stir over low heat until sugar melts. Leave aside.

3. Sizzle butter or margarine in a frying pan. Add crumbs and fry until golden and crisp. Stir in almonds and brown sugar.

4. Fill 4 tumblers with alternate layers of crumb mixture and apple purée, ending with crumbs.

5. Whip cream and milk together until thick. Pile equal amounts over each dessert and chill lightly in the refrigerator; about ¾ hour. Before serving, top each with a teaspoon of jam.

Apple and Pear Crumble
Serves 4

Perfumed with autumnal fruits, this is an extra special crumble with its topping made from brown flour and sugar, walnuts and lemon peel.

8 oz (225 g) cooking apples, peeled, quartered, cored sliced
8 oz (225 g) dessert pears (cooking ones are too hard), peeled. quartered, cored, sliced
4 to 6 oz (125 to 175 g) caster sugar, depending on sourness of fruit
1 level tsp cinnamon (optional)
1 tblsp lemon juice

Topping
6 oz (175 g) brown flour
3 oz (75 g) butter or margarine
3 oz (75 g) light brown soft sugar
2 oz (50 g) walnuts, coarsely chopped
1 level tsp finely grated lemon peel

1. Put sliced fruits into a bowl and toss with sugar, cinnamon and lemon juice.

2. Transfer to a 3 pint (1.75 litre) greased heatproof dish.

3. For crumble, tip flour into a bowl. Rub in butter or margarine finely then toss in sugar, walnuts and lemon peel.

4. Sprinkle thickly over fruit and bake ¼ hour in moderately hot oven, 375° F (190° C), Gas 5. Reduce temperature to 325° F (160° C), Gas 3 and continue to bake a further ½ to ¾ hour or until fruit is cooked and topping golden brown. Serve warm with cream or custard.

Orange Cranberry Nut Parfait
Serves 4

Half Scandinavian and half North American — a luscious sweet for winter enjoyment.

½ pt (275 ml) double cream
2 tblsp cold milk
2 oz (50 g) caster sugar
½ pt (275 ml) Orange Cranberry Nut Relish (page 66)

1. Whip cream and milk together until thick.
2. Gently stir in sugar followed by the Orange Cranberry Nut Relish.
3. Spoon into 4 dishes and add a wafer to each before serving.

Coffee Baked Bananas
Serves 4

Irresistable!

4 large bananas
1½ oz (40 g) walnuts, coarsely chopped
1 oz (25 g) butter, melted
3 tblsp coffee liqueur
2 oz (50 g) dark brown soft sugar

1. Peel bananas and slice lengthwise. Arrange in a shallow, oblong dish, placing halved cut sides down.
2. Mix all remaining ingredients together and spoon over bananas.
3. Bake ¼ hour in moderately hot oven, 400° F (200° C), Gas 6. Serve with whipped cream.

Pecan Pie
Serves 10

A United States special and one of the most favoured pies in the deep south of the country. It is unbelievably sweet so serve with plain whipped cream.

7 oz (200 g) pecan nuts
8 oz (225 g) plain flour
pinch of salt
½ level tsp mixed spice
4 oz (125 g) mixture margarine and white cooking fat or lard
3 to 4 tblsp cold water to mix

Filling
1 oz (25 g) butter or margarine, melted
6 oz (175 g) caster sugar
8 oz (225 g) golden syrup
3 Grade 3 eggs
1 tsp vanilla essence

1. Lightly toast pecan nuts. Leave on one side temporarily.
2. For pastry, sift flour, salt and spice into a bowl. Rub in fats finely then mix to a stiff dough with water.
3. Turn out on to a floured surface, knead lightly until smooth then roll out fairly thinly.
4. Use to line a 10 inch (25 cm) greased pie plate or flan ring standing on a greased baking tray.
5. Sprinkle base with pecans. Whisk rest of ingredients well together then pour into pastry case over pecans.
6. Bake ¾ hour in moderately hot oven, 375° F (190° C), Gas 5. Remove flan ring (if used), leave pie until lukewarm then cut into wedges and serve with the cream.

Walnut Pie
Serves 10

For a more economical pie, use walnut halves instead of pecans.

Bakewell Tart
Serves about 8

One of Britain's best desserts from Derbyshire. Serve it warm with cream or custard.

6 oz (175 g) plain flour
pinch of salt
3 oz (75 g) mixture of butter or margarine and lard or cooking fat
2½ to 3 tblsp cold water to mix

Filling
2 rounded tblsp raspberry jam
3 oz (75 g) butter or margarine at kitchen temperature and soft
3 oz (75 g) caster sugar
½ tsp each, almond and vanilla essence
3 Grade 3 eggs, at kitchen temperature
6 oz (175 g) cake crumbs
3 oz (75 g) ground almonds
1 tblsp milk

1. For pastry, sift flour and salt into a bowl. Rub in fats finely then mix to a stiff dough with water. Roll out fairly thinly on floured surface and use to line a 9 inch (22.5 cm) greased pie plate or flan ring standing on a greased baking tray.

2. Spread jam over base. For filling, beat butter or margarine to a light, soft cream with sugar and essences. Beat in eggs, one at a time, adding a heaped tablespoon of cake crumbs with each.

3. Fold in remaining cake crumbs and ground almonds then stir in milk. Spread smoothly into pastry case. Bake ¾ hour in moderately hot oven, 375°F (190° C), Gas 5. Leave until lukewarm then cut into wedges and serve.

Note
For a slightly lighter filling, beat egg yolks into creamed mixture. Whisk whites stiffly and fold in after adding crumbs, almonds and milk.

Apple Charlotte with Walnuts
Serves 4

A well-loved and traditional pudding, dressed-up with walnuts.

4 oz (125 g) caster sugar
4 oz (125 g) fresh white breadcrumbs
2 oz (50 g) walnuts, finely chopped
1 level tsp cinnamon or mixed spice
1 level tsp finely grated lemon peel
4 oz (125 g) butter or margarine, melted
1 lb (450 g) cooking apples, peeled, quartered, cored, thinly sliced

1. Mix sugar with breadcrumbs, nuts, cinnamon or spice, lemon peel and three-quarters of the melted butter or margarine.

2. Fill a 2 pint (1½ litre) greased pie dish with alternate layers of apples and crumb mixture, finishing with crumbs.

3. Trickle remaining butter or margarine over the top then bake until cooked, crisp and golden brown, allowing ¾ to 1 hour in moderately hot oven, 375° F (190° C), Gas 5. Serve with cream or custard.

Christmas Pudding

Makes 2 puddings, each enough for 10 to 12

Rich puddings which store well.

6 oz (175 g) fresh white breadcrumbs
6 oz (175 g) plain flour
½ level tsp salt
2 level mixed spice or the slightly stronger allspice
6 oz (175 g) dark brown soft sugar
6 oz (175 g) finely shredded suet
1½ lb (675 g) mixed dried fruit
4 oz (125 g) mixed chopped peel
2 oz (50 g) brazil nuts, coarsely chopped
2 oz (50 g) walnuts, coarsely chopped
1 oz (25 g) cashews, lightly toasted, coarsely chopped
1 level tsp each, finely grated orange and lemon peel
3 Grade 2 eggs, lightly beaten
1 tblsp black treacle
6 to 8 tblsp stout or medium sherry for mixing

1. Well-grease 2 by 2 pint (1 litre) pudding basins. Have ready 2 large saucepans.

2. Tip breadcrumbs into a bowl. Sift in flour, salt and either mixed spice or allspice.

3. Toss in sugar, suet, fruit, peel, nuts and fresh fruit peels. Using a large spoon, mix to a soft consistency with eggs, treacle and stout or sherry.

4. Divide between prepared basins, then cover securely with greased greaseproof paper or foil, making a 'pleat' so that it can open out as pudding rises.

5. Put into the 2 saucepans then add boiling water to come half way up the sides.

6. Top with lids and boil steadily for 6 hours, adding extra boiling water now and again to keep up the level and prevent pans from boiling dry.

7. Leave puddings to cool until lukewarm in their basins then turn out and cool completely. Wrap in greaseproof paper or clean cloth steeped in brandy. Overwrap in foil and store in the cool until needed.

8. Re-steam each pudding for 2 hours before serving with cream, custard, brandy butter or white sauce flavoured with rum, whisky or brandy. Alternatively, try the Nut Snow Cream on page 72.

Queen of Puddings

Serves 4

A golden-oldie, worth reviving with its topping of fluffy meringue. Serve with custard or single cream.

3 oz (75 g) bread, weighed without crusts, crumbed
1½ oz (40 g) flaked almonds, lightly toasted, fairly finely crushed
1 level tsp finely grated lemon peel
4 oz (125 g) caster sugar
1 oz (25 g) butter or margarine
¼ pt (150 ml) milk
2 Grade 2 eggs, separated
2 slightly rounded tblsp apricot or kiwi fruit jam

1. Tip crumbs into a bowl. Toss in 1 oz (25 g) almonds, lemon peel and 1 oz (25 g) caster sugar.

2. Heat butter or margarine in the milk until melted. Add to crumbs, stir well to mix and leave to stand for ½ hour.

3. Beat egg yolks into crumb mixture then spread into a 1½ pint (1 litre) greased heatproof dish. Bake ½ hour in moderate oven, 350° F (180° C), Gas 5, or until set. Remove from oven and spread with jam.

4. Whip whites to a very stiff snow. Gradually beat in two-thirds of remaining sugar. Fold in remainder with a large metal spoon.

5. Swirl thickly over pudding then sprinkle with rest of almonds. Return to oven and bake a further ½ hour when meringue should be light gold.

CAKES, BREADS AND BISCUITS

Madeleines

Makes 12

Memories of childhood brought back with these jam and coconut cakes which look like miniature castles. In the event that the individual castle pudding tins (also called dariole moulds) are not available, a variation follows.

4 oz (125 g) butter or block margarine, at kitchen
temperature and soft
4 oz (125 g) caster sugar
1 tsp vanilla essence
2 Grade 3 eggs, at kitchen temperature
4 oz (125 g) self-raising flour, sifted
about 5 slightly rounded tblsp plum jam, melted
6 rounded tblsp desiccated coconut
6 glacé cherries, halved
24 small diamond shapes, cut from angelica

1. Well-grease 12 castle pudding tins and dust insides lightly with sifted flour. If patience permits, line bases with rounds of greaseproof paper or non-stick parchment paper.

2. Beat butter or margarine, sugar and essence to a light and fluffy cream. Beat in eggs individually.

3. Using a large metal spoon, fold in flour gently. Transfer mixture to prepared tins and bake until well-risen and golden, allowing 20 to 25 minutes in moderate oven, 350° F (180° C), Gas 4.

4. Leave 5 minutes then turn out on to a wire rack and remove lining paper if used. When completely cold, cut a thin slice off the base of each (wide end) so that Madeleines stand upright without tilting.

5. Brush tops and sides with melted jam then roll in coconut, tipped on to a sheet of foil or greaseproof paper.

6. Arrange Madeleines on a serving dish (pointed ends uppermost) then top each with half a cherry and 2 diamonds of angelica.

Madeleine Cake

Cuts into 8 wedges

Make up cake mixture as directed in previous recipe. Spread smoothly into an 8 inch (20 cm) greased sandwich tin, base-lined with greaseproof paper. Bake 20 to 25 minutes in oven set to 350° F (180° C), Gas 4. Turn out and cool completely on a wire rack. Remove lining paper. Turn over and brush top and sides with melted jam. Coat all over with desiccated coconut and decorate with a border of halved glacé cherries and diamonds cut from angelica.

Austrian Almond Swirl Cakes
Makes 12

Heavenly!

7 oz (200 g) plain flour
1 oz (25 g) cornflour
8 oz (225 g) butter, at kitchen temperature and soft
3 oz (75 g) icing sugar, sifted
1 tsp vanilla essence
1 to 1½ oz (25 to 40 g) flaked almonds
6 glacé cherries, halved
extra icing sugar

1. Place 12 paper cake cases in ungreased bun tins. Set oven to moderate, 350° F (180° C), Gas 4.

2. Sift flour and cornflour into a bowl. In separate bowl, beat butter until very soft and creamy. Gradually beat in sugar followed by essence.

3. Fork in flour. Transfer mixture into an icing bag fitted with a ½ inch (1.25 cm) star-shaped tube. Pipe swirls of mixture into the 12 paper cases.

4. Press almonds gently into tops of each, leaving gaps in centres. Fill with cherry halves, cut sides down.

5. Bake for 20 to 25 minutes or until pale gold. Remove to a cooling rack, leave until cold and sift icing sugar over top of each. Store in an airtight container.

Peanut and Date Cakes
Makes 12

Rather like Fairy Cakes but different in texture and flavour through the unusual addition of salted peanuts and dates.

4 oz (125 g) self-raising flour
4 oz (125 g) butter or margarine (or mixture), at kitchen temperature and soft
4 oz (125 g) caster sugar
1 level tsp finely grated lemon peel
2 Grade 3 standard eggs, at kitchen temperature
1 oz (25 g) salted peanuts, coarsely chopped
1 oz (25 g) cooking dates, finely chopped

1. Well-grease 12 bun tins. Set oven to moderately hot, 375° F (190° C), Gas 5.

2. Sift flour into a bowl. In separate bowl, beat butter or margarine (or mixture) with sugar and lemon peel until very light and fluffy in texture.

3. Beat in eggs, one at a time, adding a tablespoon of flour with each.

4. Stir in peanuts and dates. Gently fold in rest of flour with a metal spoon then divide equally between the tins.

5. Bake 20 to 25 minutes or until well-risen and golden. Stand 5 minutes, remove cakes from tins and cool completely on a wire rack. Store in an airtight container when cold.

Dutch Butter Cake
Cuts into 8 pieces

A wonderful treat from Holland with a mouth-watering fragrance and melting texture. It resembles our own shortbread and is very much a winter speciality, usually made to celebrate the festival of St Nicholaas on December 5 and 6.

4 oz (125 g) butter, at kitchen temperature
1 level tsp finely grated lemon peel
4 oz (125 g) light brown soft sugar
½ Grade 3 egg, well beaten
4 oz (125 g) plain flour
1 level tsp cinnamon or ground ginger
single cream or evaporated milk for brushing
1 oz (25 g) flaked almonds

1. Beat butter, lemon peel and sugar together until light in texture, very creamy and much paler in colour.

2. Mix in egg then gently fork in flour and cinnamon or ginger, first sifted together.

3. Spread smoothly into a 7 inch (17.5 cm) sandwich tin and brush with the cream or evaporated milk.

4. Scatter almonds over the top and bake until golden in moderate oven, 350° F (180° C), Gas 4. Allow about 30 to 35 minutes.

5. Leave until lukewarm then cut into 8 wedges. Cool on a wire rack and store in an airtight container.

Banana and Walnut Bread
1 small

A spicy cake-cum-bread, ideal for teatime, sliced and spread with butter.

6 oz (175 g) self-raising flour
½ level tsp salt
1 level tsp cinnamon
4 oz (125 g) caster sugar
1½ oz (40 g) walnuts, chopped
2 medium ripe bananas
1 Grade 3 egg, well-beaten
1 oz (25 g) butter or margarine, melted
2 to 4 tblsp milk

1. Grease and line a 1 lb (450 g) oblong loaf tin.

2. Sift flour, salt and cinnamon into a bowl. Toss in sugar and nuts.

3. Mash bananas finely. Mix thoroughly into dry ingredients with beaten egg and melted fat, and enough milk to form a fairly stiff mixture.

4. Spoon into prepared tin and bake for 1 hour in the centre of a preheated, moderate oven, 350° F (180° C), Gas 4.

5. Turn out and cool on a wire rack. Slice when just cold.

Fruit and Nut Loaf
1 large

This is a richly fruited cake, peppered with nuts and darkened with treacle. It can be made for Christmas or any other festive occasion.

8 oz (225 g) plain flour
1 level tsp baking powder

¼ level tsp salt
2 level tsp mixed spice
6 oz (175 g) butter or block margarine, at kitchen
temperature
6 oz (175 g) light brown soft sugar
3 Grade 2 eggs, at kitchen temperature
1 level tblsp black treacle
6 oz (175 g) sultanas
6 oz (175 g) seedless raisins
2 oz (50 g) cooking dates, finely chopped
2 oz (50 g) mixed chopped peel
2 oz (50 g) brazil nuts, finely chopped
2 oz (50 g) hazelnuts

1. Line base and sides of a greased 2 lb (1 kg) oblong loaf
   tin with non-stick parchment paper.

2. Sift flour, baking powder, salt and mixed spice into a
   bowl. In separate bowl, beat butter or margarine with
   sugar until very light and creamy in consistency.

3. Beat in whole eggs, one at a time, adding a tablespoon
   of dry ingredients with each. Mix in treacle.

4. Stir in fruits and nuts then fold in remaining flour
   gently with a large metal spoon or spatula. When
   evenly combined, spread smoothly into prepared
   tin.

5. Bake 1½ hours in moderate oven, 325° F(160° C),
   Gas 4. Reduce temperature to 300°F (150° C), Gas 3,
   and continue to bake a further 1½ to 2 hours or until a
   wooden cocktail stick or metal skewer, inserted gently
   into the centre, comes out clean with no uncooked
   mixture sticking to it.

6. Remove from oven and allow to stand ½ hour for cake
   to settle. Turn out on to a wire rack and remove paper
   only if cake is going to be eaten within a week.
   Otherwise leave on.

7. Keep in an airtight container but if setting aside for a
   month or more, overwrap with greaseproof paper
   followed with a double thickness of foil. Store in the
   cool until ready for icing etc.

Almond Macaroons
Makes 16

Classic teatime biscuits with an air of exclusivity.

2 Grade 3 egg whites
4 oz (125 g) ground almonds
8 oz (225 g) caster sugar
½ oz (15 g) fine semolina
¾ tsp almond essence
½ tsp vanilla essence
water if necessary
1 extra egg white from Grade 4 or 5 egg, lightly beaten
8 whole almonds, blanched, skinned, halved

1. Line 2 lightly greased baking trays with edible rice
   paper (available from good stationers).

2. Beat egg whites to a soft foam, *not* to a stiff
   meringue.

3. Stir in almonds, sugar, semolina and essences. Mix
   thoroughly, adding 1 or 2 teaspoons water if very
   stiff.

4. Pipe or spoon 16 mounds on to prepared trays. Brush
   with some extra egg white then top each with half an
   almond, flat side down. Brush almonds with
   remaining egg white.

5. Bake Macaroons until light gold, allowing 20 to 25
   minutes in a cool oven, 325° F (160° C), Gas 3,
   reversing position of trays half way through baking.

6. Leave on trays for 5 minutes then carefully remove
   Macaroons, trimming away rice paper round each.
   Cool on a wire rack then store in an airtight container
   when cold.

Coconut Macaroons
Makes 20

More economical than ones made with almonds, these are rich in flavour and always well-liked by children.

2 Grade 3 egg whites
5 oz (150 g) caster sugar
6 oz (175 g) desiccated coconut
10 glacé cherries, halved

1. Line trays with rice paper as for Almond Macaroons.
2. Beat egg whites to a stiff snow. Stir in sugar and coconut. Mix thoroughly.
3. Place 10 rocky almonds of mixture on to each prepared tray.
4. Top with cherries. Bake until pale gold in a cool oven, 300° F (150° C), Gas 2. Allow about 35 to 40 minutes and reverse position of trays half way through baking.
5. Leave on trays for 5 minutes then carefully remove Macaroons, trimming away rice paper round each. Cool on a wire rack then store in an airtight container when cold.

Coconut Pyramids
Makes 20

Made with whole eggs instead of whites, these are temptingly golden biscuits with slightly soft middles.

2 Grade 3 eggs
8 oz (225 g) desiccated coconut
5 oz (150 g) caster sugar

1. Prepare 2 trays as directed in either of the previous 2 recipes.
2. Beat eggs until light and frothy. Stir in coconut and sugar.
3. Shape into 20 pyramids with damp hands. Stand 10 on each tray.
4. Bake until pale gold in moderate oven, 350° F (180° C), Gas 4. Allow 25 to 30 minutes and reverse position of trays half way through baking.
5. Leave on trays for 5 minutes then carefully remove Pyramids, trimming away rice paper round each.
6. Cool on a wire rack then store in an airtight container when cold.

Hazelnut Shortbread Biscuits
Makes 16 to 18

Crisp and delectable, elegant for any special occasion.

2 oz (50 g) hazelnuts, lightly toasted, skins left on
4 oz (125 g) butter or block margarine, at kitchen temperature and soft
2 oz (50 g) icing sugar, sifted
6 oz (175 g) plain flour
1 Grade 4 egg for brushing, beaten
caster sugar

1. Finely grind hazelnuts in a blender or food processor. Leave on one side temporarily.

2. Beat butter or margarine and sugar together until very light and creamy in texture.

3. Using a fork, mix in hazelnuts and flour. Draw together to form a ball. Wrap in cling film or foil and refrigerate ½ hour to firm-up.

4. Unwrap, put on to a floured surface and roll out to ¼ inch (5 mm) in thickness.

5. Cut into 16 to 18 rounds with a 2 inch (5 cm) fluted biscuit cutter, re-rolling and re-cutting trimmings to make required number of biscuits.

6. Transfer to 2 lightly greased baking trays. Prick with a fork, brush with egg and sprinkle with sugar.

7. Bake until pale gold, allowing 22 to 26 minutes in cool oven, 325° F (160° C), Gas 3, reversing position of trays half way through baking.

8. Leave to stand 5 minutes then carefully lift off trays and transfer to a wire cooling rack. Store in an airtight container when completely cold.

Shortbread Almond Biscuits
Makes 16 to 18

Make as above, substituting ground almonds for hazelnuts.

Almond Slices
Makes 12

Closely related to Macaroons, these are one of the highlights of an old English-style afternoon tea. And nothing beats the homemade version.

6 oz (175 g) plain flour
½ oz (15 g) icing sugar
pinch of salt
3 oz (75 g) mixture of butter and margarine, or butter only
2 to 3 tblsp cold water
2 to 3 level tblsp apricot jam, melted, cooled
4 oz (125 g) icing sugar, sifted
4 oz (125 g) caster sugar
6 oz (175 g) ground almonds
1 Grade 3 egg, beaten
extra white of 1 Grade 3 egg
½ tsp each, almond and vanilla essences
1½ oz (40 g) flaked almonds

1. For pastry, sift flour, icing sugar and salt into a bowl. Rub in butter and margarine (or butter only) until mixture looks like a mass of fine breadcrumbs.

2. Using a fork, mix to a stiff dough with water. Turn out on to a floured surface and knead lightly until smooth. Roll out into a 10 by 6 inch (25 by 15 cm) oblong and transfer to a lightly greased baking tray. Fork edges to decorate. Spread pastry base with jam.

3. For topping, mix both sugars with almonds then bind to a softish paste with egg, egg white and the essences.

4. Spread over pastry then sprinkle evenly with the flaked almonds. Bake until golden brown in moderately hot oven, 375° F (190° C), Gas 5. Allow about 25 minutes.

5. Cut into 12 pieces when lukewarm then cool on a wire rack. Store in an airtight container when completely cold.

Florentines

Makes 12

One of the most gracious of all biscuits, very expensive to buy. Homemade, they become a realistic and more economical proposition altogether.

3 oz (75 g) butter
4 tblsp single cream
4 oz (125 g) icing sugar, sifted
3 oz (75 g) chopped mixed peel
2 oz (50 g) glacé cherries, chopped
1½ oz (40 g) flaked almonds
1½ oz (40 g) hazelnuts, coarsely chopped
1 tsp lemon juice
1 bar (3½ oz or 100 g) plain chocolate
½ oz (15 g) butter

1. Line 2 baking trays with edible rice paper (available from good stationers).

2. Put butter, cream and sugar into a saucepan. Stand over a low heat until butter melts.

3. Take pan off heat and stir in peel, cherries, almonds, hazelnuts and lemon juice. Leave until completely cold.

4. Spoon 6 mounds of mixture, well apart as they spread, on to each prepared tray.

5. Bake until pale gold; 10 to 12 minutes in moderately hot oven, 375° F (190° C), Gas 4.

6. Lift off trays when lukewarm and trim away excess rice paper round edges. Cool on a wire rack.

7. Break up chocolate. Melt, with butter, in a basin over hot water. Spread over rice paper sides of Florentines, leave until half set then mark in wavy lines with a fork.

8. When chocolate is firm, transfer to an airtight container and store in the cool.

Hazelnut Coffee Kisses

Makes 8

Melt-in-the-mouth hazelnut meringues, filled with coffee-flavoured whipped cream, are very special indeed and may be served as an after-dinner dessert or teatime treat.

whites of 2 Grade 3 eggs
2 drops of lemon juice
5 oz (150 g) caster sugar
2 oz (50 g) hazelnuts, fairly finely ground in blender or food processor
¼ pt (150 ml) double cream
2 level tblsp caster sugar
1 tblsp liquid coffee essence (Camp) or 2 rounded tsp instant coffee dissolved in 3 tsp hot water then cooled

1. Line 1 large baking tray with foil or non-stick parchment paper. *Do not grease.*

2. Put whites into a large bowl. Add lemon juice and beat to a very stiff snow.

3. Gradually beat in two-thirds of the sugar. Continue beating until meringue is very thick and forms tallish peaks when beater or beaters are lifted out of bowl.

4. Fold in rest of sugar and hazelnuts. Spoon or pipe 16 rounds or ovals on to prepared tray.

5. Dry out for 1½ to 1¾ hours in cool oven, 225° F (110° C), Gas ¼. Take tray out of oven, turn meringues over and press a small hollow in base of each.

6. Return to oven and continue to dry out for a further ½ to ¾ hour. Cool on a wire rack.

7. Whip cream until thick. Stir in sugar and coffee. Use to sandwich meringues together to make Coffee Kisses.

Almond Coffee Kisses
Makes 8

Make exactly as previous recipe, using ground almonds instead of hazelnuts.

Note
The meringues will keep several weeks in an airtight tin but once filled, should be eaten on the same day.

Linzer Torte

Cuts into about 10 wedges

From Linz in Austria comes this glorified jam tart, densely paked with hazelnuts and filled with raspberry jam.

4 oz (125 g) hazelnuts, finely ground in blender or food processor
4 oz (125 g) plain flour
1 level tsp cinnamon
4 oz (125 g) butter, at kitchen temperature and soft
4 oz (125 g) caster sugar
1 Grade 4 or 5 egg, at kitchen temperature, separated
6 to 8 oz (175 to 225 g) raspberry jam
extra icing sugar

1. Tip nuts into a bowl. Sift in flour and cinnamon. Add butter, sugar and egg yolk.

2. Knead together to form a dough. Wrap in cling film or foil and chill in the refrigerator until firm but *not* hard; up to about 1 hour.

3. Use three-quarters of the dough to line base and sides of a 7 inch (17.5 cm) spring clip tin (the kind used for cheese cake) or the same size flan ring standing on a greased baking tray. The lining should be a little thicker than if using shortcrust pastry.

4. Fill with jam. Roll rest of dough out thinly and cut into strips. Criss-cross over top of Torte, pressing ends well into edge of dough lining the tin. If they do not hold in place, moisten with a little water.

5. Bake 45 to 55 minutes in moderate oven, 350° F (180° C), Gas 4. Torte is ready when it is a light golden brown and firm. Remove spring clip tin or flan ring.

6. Leave until lukewarm, transfer to wire cooling rack and sift icing sugar over the top. Cut into small wedges when cold (the Torte is quite rich) and serve with coffee.

Almond Linz Tort
Cuts into about 10 wedges

Make exactly as previous recipe, using ground almonds instead of hazelnuts.

Coconut and Orange Cake
Cuts into about 8 wedges

Almost tropical in flavour, this is a reliable cake for family eating.

8 oz (225 g) self-raising flour
pinch of salt
4 oz (125 g) mixture of butter or margarine and white cooking fat or lard, at kitchen temperature
4 oz (125 g) caster sugar
2 oz (50 g) desiccated coconut
finely grated peel of 1 small washed and dried orange
1 Grade 2 egg, at kitchen temperature, beaten
6 tblsp cold milk
½ tsp vanilla essence

1. Brush a 6 inch (15 cm) round cake tin with melted white cooking fat. Line with greaseproof paper and brush with more fat. Alternatively, line with non-stick parchment paper without greasing. If using a non-stick tin, line base only.

2. Sift flour and salt into a bowl. Add fats and rub in finely with fingertips. Toss in sugar, coconut and orange peel.

3. Using a fork, mix to a stiffish consistency with the egg, milk and essence, stirring briskly without beating.

4. When smoothly-combined, spread into prepared tin and bake 1¼ to 1½ hours in a cool oven, 325° F (160° C), Gas 3, or until well-risen and golden.

5. To test for doneness, push a thin metal skewer or wooden cocktail stick gently into centre. If it comes out clean with no uncooked mixture clinging to it, then the cake is ready. If not, return to oven for a further 10 to 20 minutes.

6. Leave to cool on a wire rack and peel away lining paper when cold. Store in an airtight container.

Coconut and Orange Loaf
Cuts into about 8 slices

Make as above, baking mixture in a 1 lb (450 g) oblong loaf tin.

Party Loaf
Cuts into about 8 slices

Make as the Coconut and Orange Loaf then ice top with pineapple glacé icing made by mixing 6 oz (175 g) sifted icing sugar with sufficient pineapple juice to form thickish icing. Leave undisturbed until set then decorate with halved glacé cherries, either all red or a mixture of red, green and yellow.

Walnut Cream Gateau
Serves 8

What a glorious cake this is, yet it is nothing more complex that a Victoria Sandwich made with brown flour and walnuts, filled and mounded with whipped cream and chocolate.

6oz (175 g) plain wheatmeal flour
2¼ level tsp baking powder
pinch of salt
6 oz (175 g) butter of block margarine, at kitchen temperature and soft
6 oz (175 g) caster sugar
3 Grade 3 eggs
1½ oz (40 g) walnuts, finely chopped
¼ pt (150 ml) whipping cream
1 large chocolate flake bar, crushed
½ packet (2 oz or 50 g) plain chocolate dots

1. Brush 2 by 7 inch (17.5 cm) sandwich tins with melted fat then line bases with rounds of greased greaseproof or non-stick parchment paper. If tins are non-stick, line bases only.

2. Tip flour into a bowl. Sift in baking powder and salt. Toss lightly to mix.

3. In separate bowl, whip butter or margarine and sugar to a light, soft and fluffy cream. Beat in eggs individually, adding a tablespoon of dry ingredients with each.

4. Stir in walnuts then gently fold in rest of dry ingredients with a large metal spoon.

5. Spread smoothly into prepared tins then bake until well-risen and golden brown in moderate oven set to 350° F (180° C), Gas 4. Allow 20 to 25 minutes.

6. Leave in tins 5 minutes then turn out and cool on a wire rack. Peel away lining paper when completely cold.

7. To assemble, whip cream until thick. Take off one-third and combine with crushed flake bar. Use to sandwich cakes together.

8. Spread remainder over top then decorate with the chocolate dots.

Walnut and Apricot Gateau
Serves 8 to 10

Just few simple variations and you can soon create a voluptuous gateau for parties and other festive occasions.

To assemble before serving, whip ½ pt (275 ml) double cream until thick. Stir in 2 tablespoons syrup from a 15 oz (400g) can of apricots or 2 tablespoons of apricot brandy. Drain apricots thoroughly. Save half for decoration and chop remainder. Mix about one-third of cream with the chopped apricots and use to sandwich cake together. Transfer to a serving plate and swirl rest of cream over top and sides. Decorate top edge with a border of whole apricot halves then stud here and there with walnut halves.

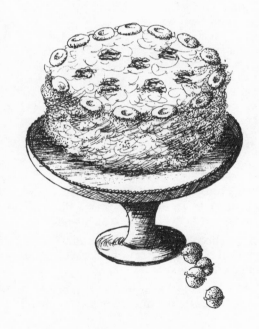

Viennese Sachertorte

In Germany and Austria, Sachertorte is seen very much as a man's cake, too dark, too rich and not light enough for the ladies to indulge in over the traditional cup of afternoon coffee! But it doesn't seem to stop them! My recipe is an adaptation of Hotel Sacher's treasured secret recipe and tastes very close to the real thing.

1 bar (3½ oz or 100 g) plain chocolate
3 oz (75 g) very lightly salted butter, at kitchen temperature and soft
3 Grade 2 eggs, at kitchen temperature
3 oz (75 g) icing sugar, sifted
2 oz (50 g) ground almonds
2 oz (50 g) plain flour, sifted
2 or 3 drops lemon juice

Coating
2 level tblsp warmed apricot jam (minus large pieces of fruit)
1½ to 2 oz (40 to 50 g) plain chocolate
2 tsp soft butter
4 oz (125 g) icing sugar, sifted
5 tsp warm water

1. For cake, brush an 8 inch (20 cm) round sandwich tin with melted butter and line base with a round of greaseproof or non-stick parchment paper.

2. Break up chocolate and put, with butter, into a basin standing over a pan of hot water. Leave until melted, stirring once or twice.

3. Separate eggs. Tip whites into a clean dry bowl. Add yolks to chocolate mixture with sugar, almonds and flour.

4. Beat egg whites and lemon juice to a stiff, peaky snow. Using a large metal spoon, fold evenly into the chocolate mixture.

5. Transfer to prepared tin and bake 35 to 40 minutes in moderate oven, 350° F (180° C), Gas 4. When ready, cake should be firm to the touch and slightly risen.

6. Leave to stand 10 minutes then turn out and cool on a wire rack.

7. Brush top and sides with apricot jam to hold crumbs in place and prevent them from getting into the icing and spoiling its appearance.

8. Break up chocolate and melt, with butter, in a basin over hot water. Stir in icing sugar and warm water.

9. Spread over top and sides of cake and leave undisturbed until set. If liked, pipe the word Sacher across the top, using extra melted chocolate.

Dundee Cake

No repetoire of cakes would be complete without this firmly-established favourite.

8 oz (225 g) plain flour
1½ level tsp baking powder
6 oz (175 g) butter or block margarine, at room temperature and soft
6 oz (175 g) caster sugar
1 level tsp finely grated orange peel
4 Grade 3 eggs, at kitchen temperature
2 oz (50 g) ground almonds
12 oz (350 g) mixed dried fruit
2 oz (50 g) chopped mixed peel
2 tblsp cold milk
1½ oz (40 g) blanched almonds, skinned, halved

1. Brush an 8 inch (20 cm) round cake tin with melted fat then line (even if non-stick) with greaseproof paper or non-stick parchment paper. If using the former, brush with melted fat.

2. Sift flour and baking powder into a bowl. In separate bowl, beat butter or margarine, sugar and orange peel to a light and fluffy cream.

3. Beat in eggs, one at a time, adding a tablespoon of dry ingredients with each. Stir in ground almonds, fruit and peel.

4. As gently as possible, fold in remaining dry ingredients alternately with milk. When evenly-combined, spread smoothly into prepared tin. Top with rings of halved almonds, flat sides down.

5. Bake 2½ to 3 hours in cool oven, 300° F (150° C), Gas 2. Cake is ready when well-risen and golden brown and when a thin metal skewer, pushed gently into centre, comes out clean with no uncooked mixture clinging to it. If not, bake cake a further 15 to 30 minutes.

6. Leave in tin until lukewarm then turn out on to a wire rack. When completely cold, store in an airtight tin without removing lining paper. Keep at least 1 week before cutting.

Christmas Cake
Serves about 20 to 25

Rich as all Christmans cakes are, this is an old friend of mine, packed with an assortment of fruit and three varieties of nuts.

8 oz (225 g) plain flour
½ oz (15 g) cornflour
½ oz (15 g) cocoa powder
3 level tsp mixed spice
8 oz (225 g) butter or half butter and half margarine, at kitchen temperaure and soft
8 oz (225 g) light brown soft sugar
finely grated peel of 1 washed and dried mandarin or clementine
2 level tsp finely grated lemon peel
1 level tsp finely grated grapefruit peel
1 tsp vanilla essence
4 Grade 2 eggs, at kitchen temperature

1½ lb (675 g) mixed dried fruit including peel
2 oz (50 g) glacé cherries, chopped
2 oz (50 g) blanched almonds, skinned, lightly toasted, chopped
1½ oz (40 g) walnuts, chopped
1½ oz (40 g) brazil nuts or hazelnuts, chopped
1 level tblsp liquid coffee essence or black treacle

1. Brush an 8 inch (20 cm) round cake tin with melted fat then line (even if non-stick) with a double thickness of greaseproof paper or non-stick parchment paper. If using the former, brush with melted fat. Tie a double thickness strip of brown paper round the outside of the tin to prevent cake from darkening too much or even burning.

2. Sift flour, cornflour, cocoa powder and mixed spice into a bowl.

3. In separate bowl, beat butter (or mixture of fats) with sugar, peels and essence until light and fluffy in texture; rather like whipped cream.

4. Beat in eggs, one at a time, adding a tablespoon of dry ingredients with each. Stir in fruits and nuts.

5. Finally mix in remaining dry ingredients with the coffee essence or black treacle. When evenly-combined, transfer to prepared tin.

6. Bake 4½ to 5 hours in very cool oven, 275° F (140° C), Gas 1. When ready, the cake should be a warm golden brown and firm to the touch. To test for doneness, push a thin metal skewer gently into centre. If it comes out clean with no uncooked mixture clinging to it, then the cake is ready. If not, return to the oven for an extra 20 to 30 minutes.

7. Keep in tin until lukewarm then turn out on to a wire rack and leave until completely cold. Do not remove lining paper. Wrap in greaseproof paper then overwrap in foil. Store from 1 to 6 weeks before covering with Almond Paste and Royal Icing see page 90.

Almond Paste (for top and sides)

8 oz (225 g) ground almonds
8 oz (225 g) caster sugar
8 oz (225 g) icing sugar, sifted
2 Grade 3 egg yolks
1 tsp each, almond and vanilla essences
3 to 4 tsp brandy, rum or sherry
melted apricot jam

1. Toss almonds with both sugars. Using a fork, mix to a softish paste with egg yolks, essences and alcohol.

2. Knead lightly on a floured surface. Brush cake (lining paper removed) all over with melted jam then cover top and sides with the Almond Paste, cut to fit. (The jam, by the way, helps the Almond Paste to stay in place.)

3. Put into a large airtight container and leave for at least 1 week before icing. This gives the paste a chance to firm-up and dry out, and prevents oil from the almonds seeping through into the white icing.

Note
If covering top only, make up half quantity of Almond Paste.

Royal Icing

3 Grade 1 or 2 egg whites
½ tsp lemon juice
1½ lb (675 g) icing sugar, sifted
1 tsp glycerine (which prevents icing from becoming rock hard)

1. Whip egg whites and lemon juice until frothy.

2. Gradually beat in icing sugar, continuing until icing forms soft peaks when beaters are lifted out of bowl.

3. Stir in glycerine then spread or swirl icing over top and sides of cake.

4. If icing has been smoothly applied, pipe on decorations to taste. If icing has a snow-like appearance, add shop bought decorations to taste; small ornaments, sprigs of holly, etc.

Notes
1. *If icing top of cake only, make up half the quantity above.*
2. *If sides are left un-iced, tie a paper frill round the cake.*

INDEX